BOOKS BY THE SAME AUTHOR

THE BURNING BUSH

THE UNCONQUERED

THE MAGIC FLIGHT

THE LORE OF THE OLD TESTAMENT

THE LORE OF THE NEW TESTAMENT

HEART UPON THE ROCK (A NOVEL)

THE LEGEND CALLED MERYOM (A NOVEL)

HOW THE GREAT RELIGIONS BEGAN

MEN AND TREES

FAIR AND WARMER

EVERYBODY'S WEATHER

HOLIDAYS AROUND THE WORLD

YOUNG HEROES OF THE LIVING RELIGIONS

THE ADVENTURES OF RAMA

THE FABLES OF INDIA

THE BIBLE FOR FAMILY READING

HOLIDAYS Around the WORLD

HOLIDAYS
Around the
WORLD

by

JOSEPH GAER

Drawings by Anne Marie Jauss

LITTLE, BROWN AND COMPANY · *Boston*

TWENTY-THIRD PRINTING

Published simultaneously
in Canada by McClelland and Stewart Limited

PRINTED IN THE UNITED STATES OF AMERICA

CONTENTS

I EVERYBODY LOVES A HOLIDAY 3

The Sun, the Moon and the Stars 4
Holidays Are History 9

II THE CHINESE HOLIDAYS 12

Say: *Yang* — Say: *Yin* 12
Spring Is Here (Li Chum)! 16
New Year's Festival 20
   The Burning of the Kitchen God 22
   New Year's Eve 24
   Fourteen Days of Celebration 27
   The Feast of the Lanterns (Teng Chieh) 28
The Pure and Bright Festival (Ch'ing Ming) 30
   Bow Before a Hero! 31
   "All Souls' Day" 32
The Dragon Boat Festival (Tuan Wu) 35
The Festival of the Tragic Lovers 38
The Birthdays of the Sun and the Moon 41
   The Birthday of the Sun 42
   The Birthday of the Moon 43
   The Man in the Moon 46
The Kiteflying Holiday (Chung Yang Chieh) 48

III THE HINDU HOLIDAYS   52

"Nine and Sixty Ways"   52
A Not-so-happy New Year's Day   56
    The House of the Alligator   57
    Dhvajaropana   58
The Holiday of Incarnations (Krishnavatara)   60
    The Three Keys   60
    The Incarnations of Vishnu (Janmashtami) 62
    The Pilgrimage to Puri   63
The Festival of the Divine Mother (Durga Puja)   65
    The Moment of Worship   68
    The Victories of Rama (Dussera) 69
The Festival of the Garland of Lights (Diwali or
  Dipavali)   71
    Rakhi Bandhana   73
    The Silver Is Red   73
    Naraka Chaturdashi   77
The Festival of Tools (Visvakarma Puja)   79
Holi (The Fire Festival)   81
    The Poet's Spring   81
    The Bonfires of Holi   83
Lucky and Unlucky Days   87

IV THE JEWISH HOLIDAYS   90

The Gift of God (The Sabbath)   90
    "Remember the Sabbath Day —"   91
    Welcome the Bride   92
    Friday, Saturday and Sunday   93
Ten Days of Repentance   94
    The Book of Life   96

Vicarious Sacrifices 96
The Day of Atonement 98
The Festival of Booths (Succoth) 100
"We Were Slaves in Egypt —" 101
The Succah 101
When the Skies Open at Midnight 103
The Eighth Day That Was Added 104
The Torah Festival 104
The Celebration of a Miracle (Hanukkah) 106
The New Year of the Trees (Hamishah Osar
Bish'vat) 109
The Feast of Esther (Purim) 110
The Queen Who Lost Her Crown 112
Contest for a Queen 113
How Haman Became Chamberlain 114
Why Haman Hated Jews 116
How Esther Saved Her People 117
The Great Celebration (Passover) 120
Scholars' Day (Lag B'omer) 125
The Pentecost (Shabuoth) 126
The Reception of the Law 127
The Grain Harvest Festival 128

V THE CHRISTIAN HOLIDAYS 130

A Merry Christmas! 130
"The Holly and the Ivy" 131
The Old Winter Solstice 133
"Silent Night —" 135
A Happy New Year! 137
Two-faced Janus 138
Fast into Feast 139

Saint Valentine's Day 141
    Wolves into Saint Valentine's Clothing 142
Easter 145
    The Stranger on the Road 147
    The Easter Parade 148
    Egg-rolling on the White House Lawn 150
May Day 152
All Saints' Day 154
    Halloween 155
    Lest We Forget! 158
Thanksgiving Day 159
Roman Catholic and Greek Orthodox Holidays 163

VI THE MOSLEM HOLIDAYS 166

Muharram 166
    The Tree at the Boundary 168
    O, Husain! O, Husain! 169
    Ashura 172
The Prophet's Birthday (Maulid an-Nabi) 172
Ramadan 175
Festival of the Sacrifice ('Id al-Adha) 179
The Pilgrimage 183
    The Awe and the Wonder 185
    The Ten Rites 187

VII OTHER HOLIDAYS 192

The Names Are Different 192
The Parsi Holidays 193
Holidays of the Jains 195

VIII THE WORLD'S NEWEST HOLIDAY 197
United Nations Day 198

Principal Holidays Observed in the United States 203

Acknowledgments 205

Index 207

HOLIDAYS Around the WORLD

I EVERYBODY LOVES A HOLIDAY

All the people on earth, regardless of whatever else they may lack, do not lack holidays. Even such primitive tribes as those who to this day do not have a written language have fasts and feasts and celebrations of every kind.

People the world over celebrate on certain days in their lives or on given days in the year.

They celebrate *family* holidays, such as birthdays and weddings, confirmations and graduations, and other events of significance to the family. These holidays are observed by each family and its friends.

They also have *national* holidays, which commemorate outstanding incidents in the nation's history, such as Independence Day and Washington's Birthday in the United

States. Each nation has its own set of national holidays which are observed by all the people of that nation.

But the most important of the world's holidays are *religious*. These are holidays recognized by all the people of a given religion regardless of where they may dwell.

And everybody, the world over, loves a holiday. They await each approaching celebration as if they were expecting a most welcome guest. Often there are special foods and fixed rituals for the holiday. And when the holiday passes, they remember it with gladness.

There are hundreds of holidays, particularly religious holidays, in the world. Most of them are very old. The names of many have been changed. Some have been shifted from one part of the year to another. Different reasons are often given for celebrating certain ones. But most of the very old holidays can be traced to the sun, the moon and the stars.

The Sun, the Moon and the Stars

About the first thing Primitive Man observed was that the sun was shining. And he noticed that it did not shine all the time. It appeared over the eastern horizon. It traveled across the dome of the sky all the way from horizon to horizon. Then the sun had set and it was dark. The darkness lasted for a long time. The Dawn Man had no way of knowing how long the darkness would last. But when, in his fear, it began to seem to him that there would never be light again, the sun appeared in the east. This was

AN OFFERING TO THE MOON GOD
After the stele of the Sumerian, Ur-Nammu

repeated over and over again, until Early Man no longer feared that the night would last forever.

The daytime and the nighttime together man called one day.

Since he had no watch with which to measure time, he

divided the day into four parts: morning, afternoon, evening and night.

But he was puzzled as to when the day really began: at sunrise or at sunset, at midnight or at noon. And the answer to this puzzle has not been agreed upon to the present day. Most people of the Western world consider that the day starts at midnight, as did the ancient Egyptians. The Jews and the Chinese, like the ancient Greeks, accept sunset as the end of the day and the appearance of the first star as the beginning of the new day. The Hindu lunar day begins at sunrise. Some ancient nations, like the Umbrians, began the day at noon, as do the astronomers and seamen of our own time.

The *length* of the day, however, was fixed from the very beginning.

Early Man also observed the moon. Unlike the sun, the moon changed practically every night. First it was a new moon that waxed larger and brighter every evening for about fifteen nights; then it began to wane and grow darker, until it was almost entirely dark. And then the new moon appeared again.

From new moon to new moon took 29½ days. This was very early named the lunar month. (The word "month" comes from the Anglo-Saxon word *mona*, meaning "moon.") And there are a number of religious holidays the world over in honor of the new moon.

The sun, Early Man observed, instead of waxing and waning, remained always the same in size and appearance, except that for a time it shone a longer period each day, and then it began to shine less and less from day to day. The light of day grew shorter and shorter, until the time arrived when day and night were the same length. This was later named the equinox.

But the light of day still continued to decrease until the nights were much longer than the days. And Primitive Man began to worry. He feared that in time the sun would go out altogether, plunging the world into everlasting darkness.

There is a legend which tells how frightened Adam and Eve were during that first winter after they had been expelled from the Garden of Eden, when they noticed the days growing shorter and shorter. Adam fasted and prayed and bathed himself in the River Gihon seven times seven days. And on the fiftieth day he noticed that the day remained unchanged. After that the days began to grow longer again.

There are many other legends which show that Early Man had this fear.

The day when the sun seems to stop on its course in the middle of the winter, and again in the middle of the summer, has been named the solstice. Every year has two equinoxes and two solstices.

We call them the vernal equinox (March 21), the summer solstice (June 22), the autumnal equinox (September 23) and the winter solstice (December 22).

Many thousands of years ago it was observed that these

dates divided the year into four parts. And the four parts of the year are called the seasons: spring, summer, autumn and winter.

In addition to his observation of the sun and the moon, Primeval Man also observed the stars of the evening sky. The most important of these were the planets Mercury, Venus, Mars, Jupiter and Saturn. Early Man believed that the sun and the moon and each of these five planets took turns in ruling over the days. First the sun ruled over a day. Then the moon took over the next day. And so on. Until each planet had ruled for a day. Then the sun took his turn again.

The days they ruled over were named very early in man's history: Sun-day (Sunday); Moon-day (Monday); Mars-day (Tuesday); Mercury-day (Wednesday); Jupiter-day (Thursday); Venus-day (Friday); and Saturn-day (Saturday).

Each nation of course had different words for the names of the planets. The English names come from the Anglo-Saxon: Sunnan-day, Monan-day, Tiwes-day, Wodnes-day, Thunres-day, Frige-day and Saeter-day.

The daytime and the nighttime was called a day. The cycle of the seven days was called a week. The cycle of each moon was called a month. The cycle of the four seasons was called a year.

Most of the holidays of the world are in some way related to the divisions of time — particularly the seasons — created by the sun, the moon and the stars.

In the very early days of man's history, people worshiped the heavenly bodies. We call that nature worship. The nature worshipers celebrated the beginning of each of the four seasons. And they either thanked the lights of the sky in the autumn for the crops the people had reaped and the good hunting they had enjoyed, or they prayed to the heavenly bodies early in the spring for the blessings of good hunting and rich crops.

Those primitive holidays of the four seasons, in different forms, exist in the world to this day.

Holidays Are History

As time went on people added many other holidays to be celebrated, each nation according to its history.

They commemorated escape from destruction by great floods. They celebrated victories won over enemies. They set aside days to remember when they were delivered from slavery. They made joyful holidays when they gained independence from tyranny. And when great religious leaders arose to teach justice and peace, these leaders too were remembered in holidays.

That is why anyone who is interested in the history and beliefs of a nation can become familiar with them through the study of that nation's holidays. But that is not always easy. For the holidays are many, and often very confusing to the stranger.

Whatever we know is easy; whatever we don't know is hard. We ourselves, for instance, would never confuse Christmas with Easter. That even sounds silly. We *know* how different they are!

But it is not so easy to know the difference between Ganga Puja and Durga Puja, or between Ch'ing Ming and Chung Yang, or between Succoth and Shabuoth. Yet to the Hindus, the Chinese and the Jews, and all the other peoples of the earth, their holidays are as well known to them as their children. They never confuse them.

The great holidays of the world are like children in still another way: though the holidays of each nation seem different, they are actually very much alike. They differ in their outer appearance but they are similar in spirit.

All the people of the earth, for instance, celebrate the gathering of the harvest. The Chinese call the festival the Birthday of the Moon; the Jews call it Succoth; the Hindus call it Kojagari Purnima; and in some countries of the Western world it is called Harvest Home. These festivals take place at different times because the crops ripen at different times in different climates.

But the *spirit* of all these harvest festivals is still the spirit of thanksgiving.

When we study the holidays of the world we find that in their *origins* most of them are related to the early nature-worshiping festivals; and in their *spirit* they all express either thankfulness (to the gods, to the laws of nature, or to the ancestors) for the dew of the sky and the fat of the land, or solemn prayers to the same forces for a good year, good health, children and wealth.

The study of holidays is like the study of languages. The better we come to know other languages, the better we understand the people who use them. For we understand not only the meaning of the words but, what is more important, we begin to understand the spirit of the people. The holidays of the nations, like their languages, teach us first how they differ from us and, when we come to know them, how much like us they actually are.

For when we understand the spirit of the holidays of the nations it becomes clear to us that all of them aspire to what all the great religions of the world call the Brotherhood of Man.

II THE CHINESE HOLIDAYS

Say: *Yang*—Say: *Yin*

Most Chinese holidays rest on three beliefs:

1. The first is the belief that the world is ruled by Two Creative Principles: *Yang* and *Yin*. *Yang* is the positive, or male, principle; and *Yin* is the negative, or female, principle.

A mountain, for instance, is *Yang;* and a valley is *Yin*. A fixed star is *Yang;* and a moving star is *Yin*. An odd number is *Yang;* and an even number is *Yin*. A god in heaven is *Yang;* and the soul of an ancestor is *Yin*.

Every *Yang* has its *Yin*.

The Great Yang of the World (T'ai Yang) is the

sun; and the Great Yin of the World (T'ai Yin) is the moon.

(If you wish to write down these Two Creative Principles in Chinese, you have only to draw a straight unbroken line like this: —— and then draw the same line broken in the middle like this: — —. Now you have written two Chinese words: *Yang* and *Yin*.)

2. The second belief is that the sun and the moon and all the stars in heaven are the dwelling places of the gods, the Eight Immortals, the heroes, and the souls of ancestors. Nobody ever really dies. The souls simply go up to dwell with the gods on the stars in heaven.

3. The third belief is that the gods, the Eight Immortals, the heroes and the souls of ancestors rule the world. But they do not decide whether we receive good or evil from them. The people on the earth decide that. If we take care of our families, respect our elders, live in peace with our neighbors and shun corruption, then the gods and all the other dwellers of the planets are pleased, and they take good care of us. Otherwise we displease the gods and ancestors and there is nothing for them to do but punish us.

The Chinese, therefore, have studied all the heavenly bodies to find out what powers each star or group of stars has over human affairs. They are the world's greatest astrologers. The devout Chinese would not dream of doing anything important without first consulting the stars. He would not start to build a house, sow a field, get married, or even bury a member of the family, without first finding out from the stars the lucky day and the proper hour for such an undertaking.

Of all the heavenly bodies the most important to the Chinese are the sun and the moon, and the five planets: Mercury, Venus, Mars, Jupiter and Saturn. Of course they do not call them by their Latin names, but by their Chinese names: T'ai Yang (the sun), T'ai Yin (the moon), Shui Hsing (Mercury), Chin Hsing (Venus), Huo Hsing (Mars), Mu Hsing (Jupiter), T'u Hsing (Saturn).

Though the Chinese were probably the first people on earth to divide time into the seven-day periods which we call weeks, they have no names for the days of the week. Nor is there a day of rest each week. For the Chinese have no Sabbath Day.

But they do have many holidays.

Their holidays do not fall every year at the same time on fixed days, but they shift back and forth every three years. That is because the Chinese year is divided into twelve months of 29 and 30 days. This makes the Chinese lunar year only 354 days. So every three years they simply add a month to allow the lunar year to catch up with the travels of the sun.

The Chinese have no names for the days of the week; and they have no names for their months, either. They simply count time by the moon and say that a certain holiday comes on the fifth day of the Fifth Moon, or the seventh day of the Seventh Moon.

Each Moon (or month), however, has a nickname. The

First Moon is called the Holiday Moon. Then comes the Budding Moon, the Sleepy Moon, the Peony Moon, the Dragon Moon, the Lotus Moon, the Moon of Hungry Ghosts, the Harvest Moon, the Chrysanthemum Moon, the Kindly Moon and the White Moon. The Twelfth Moon, coming at the worst part of the winter, is nicknamed the Bitter Moon.

And since practically everything in China is represented by symbols, the twelve Moons are also represented by flowers, each an emblem of something feared or something desired. The plum blossom represents the First Moon, and stands for the promise of a long life. The remaining months are represented by the peach blossom, the peony, the cherry blossom, the magnolia, the pomegranate, the lotus, the pear, the mallow, the chrysanthemum, the gardenia and the poppy; each, in turn, promising marriage, love, beauty, sweetness, children, and so on.

Because of the beliefs of the Chinese, and the way they count time, practically all Chinese holidays are devoted to the worship of their ancestors and heroes; and at the same time they are also devoted to the worship of the sun, the moon, the stars, and the seasons these create.

Most Chinese believe in three religions: Confucianism, Buddhism and Taoism. They believe all three at the same time. Confucianism, or the teachings of Confucius, they follow as a code of ethics. Buddhism, or the teachings of Gautama Buddha, they accept as a philosophy of life. And Taoism, or the teachings of the old philosopher, Lao-tse, with its mysteries and its ideas of the supernatural, they follow in their customs, their manners and in many of their beliefs.

But most of the Chinese holidays go back to the times before Lao-tse; before the teachings of the Buddha reached China from India; before the days of Kung Fu-tse, whom we call Confucius. They go back to the days when the Chinese, like most early nations, were nature worshipers.

Ancestor worship and nature worship are reflected in all the Chinese holidays of today.

Spring Is Here (Li Chum)!

Everybody loves spring. And practically every nation on earth celebrates the arrival of spring.

Each nation or religion gives the holiday a different name. Most of them give a different reason for celebrating, a reason that has nothing to do with spring.

But the Chinese call their nature holidays exactly what they are.

They have a holiday late in February called Yu Shui. It means "spring showers." That is what the holiday is about.

Three weeks later, early in March, they celebrate Ching Che. This means "The insects are stirring." And it is the time for everybody to go out to kill insects and curse the sparrows that destroy the seeds. The people eat sweets and make a game of killing insects.

The longest day in the year, in June, is celebrated with a holiday called H'sia Chih, the summer solstice. And early in October comes a rather sad holiday, called Han Lu. This means "The dew grows cold." It is the holiday which marks the end of summer, and on this day the Chinese treat the summer as a departing guest.

CEREMONIAL PLOWING

But the happiest and most widely celebrated nature holiday is Li Chum — "Spring is here!"

On this day, usually early in February, great plowing ceremonies take place in the farm districts. In the rural areas a representative of the government, in his most resplendent official robes, arrives early in the morning at an appointed field where a plow and oxen (or water buffaloes) are waiting near a small shrine. There he is greeted by the farmers and their families. The official makes an offering of sweets and fruit to the god of spring and the god of husbandry. Incense is burned on the altar, and the official plows the first furrow in the field. In the towns and cities long and colorful processions are arranged to welcome spring. In these processions flags and banners are carried, as in most Chinese gatherings and parades. The people also carry fresh and artificial flowers.

But most prominent of all in the festival is the ox or water buffalo, which is the Chinese symbol of spring and new life in the field. Small clay images of the buffalo are carried by the paraders and a huge image of a buffalo is borne through the streets with great reverence. The frame of this buffalo is made of bamboo, for bamboo is called "the friend of China" and is a symbol of long life. When the bamboo frame is finished, it is taken to be covered with papers of five different colors: black, white, red, green and yellow. These five colors represent what the Chinese consider the five elements of the world: fire, water, metal, wood and earth. They also represent the five kinds of grain grown in China, the five kinds of weather conditions, and the five planets that rule the five elements of this world. Five is, indeed, the most important number in Chinese symbolism.

By looking at the five-colored buffalo in the procession the people can tell what kind of weather to expect during the coming year. For when the bamboo frame of the buffalo is finished it is taken to a blind man, or a blind-folded man, who pastes on the paper. He is given an equal number of pieces of each of the five colors all mixed up together. He pastes on the papers, picking them up at random. But of course he cannot see their color.

When he finishes his work the buffalo is taken out for the procession. The people look at it carefully: if it has more red than any other color, the summer will be very hot; if yellow is most in evidence it will be very windy; if the outstanding color is white, the weather will be bad; if black, the weather will be good; and if green, rain is to be expected.

In this procession of Li Chum there are no spectators. Everybody is in the parade. Old and young, rich and poor, merchant and craftsman, priest and government official — all take part in the procession. That is, all except soldiers and military officers. It would seem that the gods who dwell in the heavens, the heroes and the souls of the ancestors, do not like to see soldiers in the spring. It is a bad omen. And soldiers are everywhere forbidden from parading on this day which promises the coming of spring.

When the procession reaches the temple all the clay images of the buffalo are destroyed. And the bamboo buffalo is ceremoniously burned so that his spirit may go up to heaven to plead for a prosperous season for all the people.

After the procession the people return to their homes and continue the celebration. Candles are lighted and incense is burned. In the most prominent place in the house plates with five kinds of fruit or five kinds of seeds are arranged as a sacrifice to the gods.

Some of the people go off to witness the centuries-old plays given traditionally on this holiday. Others go to plum-blossom parties. And many people go to weddings, for the first day of spring is considered a very lucky time for a wedding and many are the weddings of this night. A wedding in China is a colorful event, full of ritual and joyful music. Those who are not guests at a wedding gather in the streets or near a bridegroom's home to watch the ceremonies.

Li Chum is a very joyous holiday.

New Year's Festival

Of all the Chinese holidays, the New Year's Festival is the most important and also the merriest. No other holiday of any other people in the world quite compares with it. The Chinese have no Sabbath Day, and their New Year's celebration seems to be many Sabbaths rolled into one. Then, too, New Year's is also a birthday celebration for every Chinese. For, regardless of the actual date on which a Chinese child is born, he is considered exactly a year old on New Year's Day. In addition, on this holiday the Chinese rejoice that winter is practically over.

For the Chinese, the new year arrives with the first day of the First Moon, the Holiday Moon, which is usually early in our month of February.

Long before the holiday arrives, preparations begin for festivities that are to last for fifteen days. Every home is thoroughly cleaned. Walls are whitewashed. The five areas ruled over by the household gods are remembered — the doors, the hearth, the living room, the front gate and the walk are all attended to; and those who can afford it re-lacquer in red their doors and front gates. The color red on gates and doors is intended to keep the evil spirits away.

After the cleaning comes the decoration of the home with the five lucky signs of happiness. These are inscriptions on little red pieces of paper which are attached to window sills and door frames and used as charms to attract good luck and to ward off evil. And while the cleaning goes on, the lanterns are made ready, firecrackers are bought, food for the dead and the living is baked and cooked, flags and banners are inspected and set in place. And those who are to take part in the annual Dragon Play must get their costumes ready and rehearse their music and their parts in this religious-historical pageant.

And, of course, everybody is busy trying on new clothes and new shoes. All who can afford it buy new clothes for the entire family for the new year. But even the poorest buy new shoes; for it is bad luck to step down on the ground on New Year's Day into old shoes.

The Burning of the Kitchen God

Several days before the new year, every family in China prepares a farewell feast for T'sao Wang, Prince of the Oven, or God of the Kitchen, before he leaves for heaven to report on the behavior of the family during the past year. The children are very busy at this time making beautifully decorated paper chariots, in which the Kitchen God will ride on his journey to heaven.

The paper image of the Kitchen God, who rules from a bamboo shrine in the kitchen during the entire year, is taken down by the head of the family. The image is placed on an altar and before him is set an offering of sweets. Usually five kinds of sweet foods are placed before him. And after the proper ritual the lips of the Kitchen God are smeared with honey, so that when he reaches heaven he will report to the Jade Emperor only sweet things about the family.

Then the Kitchen God is taken into the courtyard, and while prayers are said the image is burned, along with the paper chariots made by the children. For, it is believed, only in fire and smoke can a god go up to heaven. The children then rush to throw dry peas and beans on the roof so that everyone may hear the hoofs of the horses carrying T'sao Wang off to heaven.

And when the paper has turned into ashes the children set off firecrackers to wish their Kitchen God a happy

THE KITCHEN GOD

After a popular picture

farewell, and to frighten away the evil spirits until he returns to their home again. For, as everyone in China knows, fire, the color red, and loud noises are feared by the evil spirits that are everywhere.

Just before the new year arrives, the Kitchen God returns. The master of the house, who alone may worship at T'sao Wang's shrine, brings out a new image of the Kitchen God, usually printed on rice paper in red, green and bright yellow. He places it ceremoniously in the shrine and utters the traditional prayers.

Then the knives and all the sharp kitchen cutlery, which were hidden when the Kitchen God was sent up to heaven (so that the evil spirits could not injure the family's good luck), are returned to their places.

New Year's Eve

Finally all the preparations are complete, and all is ready for the great festivity of the year.

Early on the day before the first day of the First Moon, the men go out to settle their debts. For the new year must be faced with a clean slate. Anyone who has not paid all debts before New Year's Day loses face, which in China means that he is disgraced. Shops are open and customers crowd around the owners, each waiting to settle his account.

On New Year's Eve the members of the family gather together to say a solemn good-by to the old year. The head of the family dresses up in his finest gown, lights the incense on the altar-table that is found in each home, and seals all the doors with paper seals. He sends up a prayer and makes an offering to the God of Heaven and Earth;

SEALING THE DOOR

then he makes a similar offering to the family ancestors. Now the whole family approaches the gaily bedecked table for the last meal of the year.

The table is usually covered with a red cloth decorated with flowers. In the center stands a dish with offerings of rice, vegetables, tea and wine. Red candles are lighted and incense is burning. Sprays of cedar are often placed with the offerings. In a bowl near the offerings are a number of oranges, with an almanac for the coming year placed carefully on a stack of paper money, for good luck.

The last meal of the year is eaten in a leisurely fashion, since practically everyone stays up until midnight to say good-by to the old year and to welcome the new year.

The reception given the new year in China is unlike the New Year's Eve celebrations of the Western world. There, at the approach of midnight, all shops are locked and streets are completely deserted. Everyone is at home. The doors are locked and sealed with good-luck papers. If there should be a knock on a door, no one would answer.

Exactly at midnight begins a ceremonious exchange of New Year's greetings between the members of each family. They do not shout. They do not embrace each other. They do not lift glasses in toasts. Instead, the head of the family and his wife seat themselves as rigid as statues, and the rest of the family, in their order of age, perform a ceremony called *K'o T'ou*, or kowtow, which means "touch the ground with the forehead." As they rise from the kowtow they congratulate their elders very formally and wish them a happy new year. The children are given gifts of coins in little red envelopes which bear the inscription, printed in silver or gold: "New Happiness for the New Year!" Then the family retires.

But soon afterwards, long before the sun rises, long

before the cock crows or the horse stamps its feet in the stable, the people awake to break the seals on the doors and to devote the day to worship of their ancestors.

On this day it is bad luck to tell a lie, to raise one's voice or to use indecent language. The very polite and well-behaved Chinese are on this day even more soft-spoken and gentle, and are on their best behavior.

On this day the streets of Chinese towns and cities are deserted. Few people leave their homes, and then only if it is absolutely necessary.

Fourteen Days of Celebration

On the second day of the new year the streets become filled with holiday crowds. Neighbors and friends bow to each other when they meet, and congratulate each other formally.

"*Kung-hi!*" say the younger. "I wish you joy!"

"*Sui-hi!*" answer the elder. "May joy be yours!"

And the days of merriment and feasting are on. Friends are visited with New Year's cards; sometimes baskets of oranges and other fruit are brought with the greetings. Guests are entertained with music, fruit and sweets.

On the third and fourth days it is customary for children to go in groups from house to house, singing holiday songs in the streets, and waiting for the doors to open so that they may be rewarded with rice cakes, round as the

family circle and sweet as peace. Or they are given oranges
as good wishes for their happiness; or other fruit and sweets
that signify joy, peace and long life.

On these days, too, bands of musicians appear in the
streets with groups of actors; and for two weeks they roam
about, early and late, presenting the pageant of the season,
the Dragon Play.

The Feast of the Lanterns (Teng Chieh)

The New Year celebrations end with the Feast of the
Full Moon, or the Feast of Lanterns.

On the last three evenings of the New Year Festival,
people hang lighted lanterns on their porches and in their
gardens. Lanterns of different shapes and colors appear before the temples and in the streets.

And on the night of the fifteenth day of the First Moon
a great celebration is held, called Teng Chieh. This is the
Feast of Lanterns. How this holiday began, more than two
thousand years ago, no one really knows, though it is
claimed that it was originally a solemn ritual to the First
Cause from which came the Two Creative Principles.
But now the Feast of Lanterns is a very gay celebration
given over mostly to amusement of the young.

On the evening of this festival, people come out into
the streets with lanterns to take part in a great parade.
Usually the parade is headed by a huge dragon, the Chinese

symbol of goodness and strength. The dragon is made of bamboo and covered with silk or paper. Often the dragon is over a hundred feet long and requires a hundred men and boys to carry it on their shoulders. The huge dragon

THE DRAGON CARRIED IN PROCESSIONS

is borne along with only the moving feet of the men and boys showing.

As the parade of the lanterns, led by the giant dragon, makes its way through the streets, the watching crowds set off strings of firecrackers, and the noise is greater than at a Fourth of July celebration.

The hilarity of the evening is carried over to the next day. But when the Feast of the Lanterns is over, the fifteen-day New Year's holiday comes to an end.

The Pure and Bright Festival (Ch'ing Ming)

The Chinese must love spring very much: for they celebrate its arrival twice.

First they rejoice in the *promise* of spring in the festival Li Chum, which comes early in the Holiday Moon or late in the Bitter Moon, when it is still very cold and the nights are very long.

But on the third day of the Third Moon — the Sleepy Moon — the Chinese celebrate the coming of *real* spring in a holiday named Ch'ing Ming, which means "the pure and bright festival."

The date of this holiday is quite fixed. For it comes exactly 106 days after the sun in the heavens seemed to have stopped still, and the days were very, very short, and the nights were very, very long — the time of the winter solstice. After that date, the days begin to grow longer and the nights shorter.

Exactly 106 days after the winter solstice, the Chinese believe, spring has formally arrived. By that time the cold, dark earth wears a cover of green. The branches of the bare trees begin to swell with buds and tender leaves. The willows, the symbols of spring and the badge of meekness, attire themselves in silvery velvet. The swallows, fast as lightning, return from the south to build their nests, and the wild geese fly north in high formations. The early flowers of spring are out, and the air vibrates with the hum of insects. The time has come to celebrate Ch'ing Ming.

Bow Before a Hero!

Three days before Ch'ing Ming, early in April, all the fires in the kitchens of China are allowed to go out and no new fires are started. Little food is eaten during these days; and what is eaten, is eaten cold.

These days are known as Han Shih, or "cold food."

There are many reasons given for the days of cold food before the Pure and Bright Festival. And this is the reason given most often:

Long ago, over 2300 years ago, there lived in the Dynasty of Chou a great and noble Lord of Tsin. He was a good ruler and the people loved him. One day the Lord of Tsin gathered a number of trusted servants and good companions and started out on a long and dangerous journey.

On the way a great misfortune befell them. They were stranded in an uninhabited place and threatened by death from hunger. But one loyal companion so loved the sovereign lord that he gave his own life to spare Lord Tsin from starvation.

When the travelers had finally been rescued, and had returned home, the Lord of Tsin decreed that every year the people should honor the memory of his noble companion.

"Let his memory be honored," said the decree, "by lighting no fires in the home for three days and by eating only cold food during these days."

Then the Lord of Tsin caused a memorial tablet to be set up to this noble ancestor, before which all future generations would come to worship the Patriot of Tsin.

And that is how the Patriot of Tsin is honored and remembered to this day.

"All Souls' Day"

Early on the day of the Pure and Bright Festival, the people of China prepare to visit the graves of their families and ancestors. Each family owns its own burial ground outside the village or the city wall. Burial grounds are usually on hillsides; and the families stream out of the towns and villages and cities to the hillsides for the greater part of the day. There they sweep the graves of fallen leaves and repair whatever damage was done during the winter to the burial mounds and the stone altar-tables.

Even in the burial grounds the Chinese show their respect for their elders. There is a place where the head of the family may be buried; a place for married people with children; a place for childless couples; a place for those who died in childhood or babyhood. The Chinese would consider it a bad omen, and very disrespectful, to bury a young child in the honored place reserved for an elder in the family!

And on this great spring festival they honor the dead, each according to his age and the place of honor he held in the family. After the burial ground has been put in order, the graves are decorated with willow sprigs. On each grave are secured two white papers, which represent paper money. Then offerings of food are set before the souls of the departed members of the family.

Rich people serve a great feast in many courses to the departed souls. The poor offer whatever they can afford. But all are careful to make their offerings in *even* numbers; just as they are careful to make their offerings to the gods in *odd* numbers. That is because the gods are *Yang;* and the souls of people are *Yin.* And the principles of *Yang* and *Yin* must never be ignored.

Whether the offering to the dead is a poor man's handful of grain or a rich man's feast, the living whisper humbly in their prayer:

"We have come to you with this offering of food. It is poor and insufficient. But we implore you to forgive us and come, eat of what we have brought you."

After a little while, after the dead have had a chance to eat of the *spiritual* part of the food brought them, the family sits down to a picnic on the burial ground, eating the *material* part of the food, which the dead cannot eat.

On this day it is the duty of every person to visit the family burial ground and pay his respects to the dead. Families that are far from home and cannot reach the burial ground obtain two large paper bags decorated with two human figures in flowery robes. Between the figures there is a space in which the head of each family puts down neatly all the names of those buried in the family graveyard. Then he fills the bags with paper money, in even numbers. These he places on the family altar, beside the offerings of fruit, sweets and tea. He performs the ritual of ancestor worship and whispers the prayers to the dead just as if he were at the family burial ground.

When he is through, the bags with the paper money are taken outside and burned. This is done to free the souls of the dead who have come to be with their kin on this day. While the bags and paper money burn, the head of the household kowtows in the direction of the family graves.

After the feasts on the burial grounds, the people return to their homes, start new fires in their stoves, and decorate the houses with willow branches, as the symbols of spring.

Though Ch'ing Ming is the Chinese Memorial Day, it is not a sad or even solemn day. It is celebrated with respect; but also joyously, as on a day set aside for a great picnic.

On this day it is also customary for government officials to plant trees in public ceremonies, as is done on Arbor Day in our country. And so the holiday that celebrates the coming of real spring, which is also known as the First Feast of the Dead, turns out to be also the Tree Planting Festival.

Ch'ing Ming is therefore a three-in-one holiday.

The Dragon Boat Festival (Tuan Wu)

On the fifth day of the Fifth Moon — the Dragon Moon — the Chinese celebrate solemnly, and in a strange way, the memory of a beloved patriot who died nearly 2300 years ago.

The name of the patriot was Ch'u Yuan of Ying. He was an honest man who hated corruption. But, alas, the government of his day was very corrupt. Ch'u Yuan thought that to see what is wrong and not to try to right it is evil. And he started out to expose the corruption of the rulers of his day in the province of Ying.

One of the politicians, angered by Ch'u Yuan's disclosures, falsely accused the honest patriot of a very dishonorable act. The angered politician was a princeling. And in those days there was nothing an ordinary citizen could do to prove his innocence, when falsely accused by a prince, but throw himself into the river, which is what Ch'u Yuan did.

The people of Ying loved Ch'u Yuan and knew that he was innocent of the act charged against him by the politician. They wanted to show that they loved him and considered him innocent. So they organized searching parties to go out on the river looking for his body.

They decorated their boats with flags and, striking gongs to keep the evil spirits away, they raced down the river.

Each boat tried to be the first to reach the place where Ch'u Yuan was drowned, so that they could be the first to make an offering of rice and sweets to the soul of the departed hero.

Whether the body of the drowned man was ever found or not is nowhere recorded. But the story of his death traveled from Ying to all the provinces of the many kingdoms. And ever since then the memory of the patriot who opposed corruption is celebrated every year with boat races.

On the morning of the fifth day of the Fifth Moon, all the homes are decorated with pungent-smelling herbs, hung from the door tops and window sills. People dress in their best clothes. Young and old go down to the lakes or the nearest rivers to watch the boat races.

The boats are usually very long — over a hundred feet — but fairly shallow and narrow. The bow is carved as a dragon's head, painted and gilded, and the stern appears as a dragon's tail, just as colorful as the head. Each boat is decorated with many flags. In addition to the rowers, there are people in each boat who carry gongs.

The boats are lined up. The signal for the start is given. All the gong-bearers begin to strike their gongs to encourage the rowers. The crowds along the shores cheer the racers on. The rowers strain to pull out ahead of those near them. For all of them want to be first at the place where Ch'u Yuan drowned, ever so many centuries ago.

But why are the boats in the shape of dragons? And why

THE DRAGON BOAT FESTIVAL

is this day known as the Dragon Boat Festival? For this, too, there is a good explanation.

In the beginning, so the Chinese believe, nothing existed but the Two Principles, *Yang* and *Yin*. Then the first man, whom they call P'an Ku, was created. P'an Ku, the Chinese Adam, was a powerful man. His groan created the thunder and his breath created the wind. The gods directed P'an Ku to bring order out of chaos. P'an Ku was a very strong man, but he could not do all that without help. And so he was given the dragon, the tortoise, the phoenix, the white tiger and the unicorn as assistants.

P'an Ku divided the world into four parts:

To the dragon, faithful protector and benign guardian, he gave the eastern part from which comes spring; to the tortoise, long-lived and enduring, he gave the northern part from which comes winter; to the phoenix, the joyful and the kindly, he gave the south from whence comes the summer; and to the white tiger, full of courage and independence of spirit, he gave the west wherefrom comes autumn. And he commanded the unicorn to help all the others whenever they were in need of help.

But of all these the dragon found greatest favor in the eyes of the people of China. For the dragon alone has the power to make itself invisible. And the dragon is as good as he is strong. And, if he pleases, he has the power to bring rain when rain is needed.

That is why, while the people remember the good patriot Ch'u Yuan in their festival, they try at the same time to put themselves in the good graces of the dragon, the ruler of spring and the giver of rain. For it is summer now, and the people pray for rain so that their crops may not fail.

In this way the Chinese make the Dragon Boat Festival a double holiday.

Every so often there are politicians who try to prohibit the boat races, hoping that the people will forget their beloved patriot Ch'u Yuan who would rather die than tolerate corruption. But the people do not want to forget him any more than they wish to anger the dragon during the Dragon Moon. And so they continue to celebrate this day as a double holiday.

The Festival of the Tragic Lovers

In the constellation of the Eagle there is a bright star called Altair, known as the Falling Star. Altair came down to the earth many centuries ago, the Chinese believe, disguised as a herdsman, and he assumed the name of Ci'ien Niu.

One day, as Ci'ien Niu pastured his cows near a stream, he heard one cow say to him in a human voice:

"Altair, Son of Heaven, can you see those seven maidens bathing in the stream? One of them is Vega or Chih Nu, the brightest star in the constellation of the Harp. She and her six sisters, who weave the garments of the gods, have left their looms and have come down to bathe in this stream."

Altair turned toward the stream and he saw Vega, more beautiful than any maiden in heaven or on earth. And Altair took Vega's clothes away so that she would be earthbound.

After that the herdsman and the weaving maiden met many times, and they fell in love. They were married, and for three years lived blissfully together.

Meanwhile the loom in heaven was neglected and no garments were woven for the gods. This so angered the gods that they ordered both Vega and Altair to return to their heavenly abodes. But the bright star of the Harp and the brightest star of the Eagle were so much in love with each other that they continued to neglect their heavenly duties.

Then the Heavenly Mother-in-law took out her great silver hairpin, and with one swift movement drew a line across the heavens between Vega and Altair. Immediately a turbulent river separated the lovers, and they were forced to live on opposite sides of the river, called the Milky Way.

For a long time the two lovers grieved, Vega on her side and Altair on his side of the silver river. And their grief did not diminish with the passing of time.

Finally the story of their grieving reached the ears of the Jade Emperor on his heavenly throne, and he, in his mercy, relented and decreed that on one day each year, on the seventh day of the Seventh Moon, the lovers might be reunited.

But there is no bridge for the lovers to cross. So very early on the morning of that day in the year all the birds of joy (as the magpies are called in China) fly up to the skies and, wing to wing, create a bridge for Vega to cross to her lover Altair.

On one of the famous Ming vases the story of these two lovers is beautifully depicted. And it shows that at the end of the day, when the lovers must part for another year, they weep so bitterly that their tears come down to earth in torrents of rain.

When the seventh day of the Seventh Moon comes round, the day when the unhappy lovers are to be reunited, the people of China celebrate joyously. Bowls of fruit and vegetables are placed in the brightest part of the house as an offering to Vega and Altair. Sweets are eaten. And many stories are told.

In the cities and towns the people go to the theater to see the classical play, *Crossing the Milky Way*, presented only on this holiday. And, as in most of the Chinese classical plays dealing with the triumph of good over evil or of love over hate, the play ends happily.

The women in particular love this holiday. For it is believed that any woman who wishes to become expert in needlework will have her wish come true if she spends this day in threading a needle and practicing her skill.

That is why this holiday in the Moon of Hungry Ghosts is also called the Threading of the Needle Holiday.

THREADING NEEDLES
Based on a Chinese print

The Birthdays of the Sun and the Moon

The sun is called in China the King of the Day and the Lord of Light, Heat and Power.

The moon is called the Queen of the Night, and she

rules over the coolness of the night, the clouds, the dew and the rain.

Of all the kings and queens in the world, the sun and the moon are the happiest couple. They never quarrel. They never interfere with each other. They never do anything to offend each other. They never fail each other. And the Queen of the Night always follows the King of the Day modestly, at the proper distance, shining in the reflected glory of her consort.

The Birthday of the Sun

The birthday of the King is celebrated early in the year, on the second day of the Second Moon when, so the Chinese say, the plants on the mountains turn into jade.

That is another way of saying that the Red Cock who dwells in the sun has spread his wings and announced: "The night of winter shall from this day on be shorter than the day of spring!"

The Festival of the Sun begins in the home. Long before noon, five saucers are filled with cakes and sweets and placed before the sun on the stone altar in the courtyard. Red candles, in odd numbers, are lighted; and beside them are placed incense and paper money. After a brief service, in which the male members of the family perform the ceremony of *K'o T'ou* (or kowtow), the paper money is burned with incense. Then the children are given red sweets in the shape of cocks.

After that the families go to their temples to burn incense to the sun, or they take part in many gay public games. In some parts of China cockfights are held, since the Red Cock is the dweller of the sun who wakes mankind each morning to its duties of the day.

And on this day priests in the temples and wandering storytellers in the market places, relate again the wonderful story of Creation. They tell of the time when the first man, P'an Ku, was created out of the shapeless mass that floated like sea-jelly on the dark waters. On the palm of P'an Ku's left hand was inscribed: T'ai Yang (the sun); and on the right appeared: T'ai Yin (the moon). The first man stretched out his left hand and commanded the King of the Day to appear. Then he stretched out his right hand and commanded the Queen of the Night to appear. And, as P'an Ku repeated a charm seven times, the Royal Twain ascended to their places in the heavens, banishing forever the darkness that had existed before Creation.

This is the story young and old never tire of hearing every year, on the second day of the Second Moon, called the Budding Moon, when the Festival of the Sun is gaily celebrated.

The Birthday of the Moon

On the fifteenth day of the Eighth Moon, called the Harvest Moon, the rule of the sun begins to wane. From that day on, the days begin to grow shorter and cooler; the nights grow longer; and once again autumn is in the air.

On the night of the fifteenth day the Queen of Heaven is at her brightest, as if her face had been highly polished; and it is without any blemish. It is also the only night in the year, the Chinese believe, when the moon is perfectly round. The Queen of Heaven is celebrating her birthday.

The Birthday of the Moon is one of the happiest and one of the most important holidays of China. For it is really several holidays in one.

The Birthday of the Moon arrives when the harvests are in and the people all over China celebrate the "Harvest Home" or "Thanksgiving." They are grateful to their gods and to their ancestors for the crops of the summer that will provide for them throughout the winter. It is a season for rejoicing.

The fifteenth day of the Harvest Moon is also known as T'wan Yuan Chieh: the Festival of Reunion, or the Festival of Liberation. For, many centuries ago, the Mongols invaded China and took the emperor prisoner. Then the people arose against their conquerors and overcame Mongolia in turn. On the fifteenth day of the Harvest Moon the people liberated their emperor and placed Mongolia under Chinese rule. And that event is remembered on this day.

But most important of all is the celebration of the Moon's Birthday.

Long before the holiday arrives, cakes are baked, round as the moon, made of pale-yellow flour, decorated with red, yellow, green, and sometimes with gold leaf. Houses are cleaned and decorated with pictures of the Moon Rabbit and the Moon Toad. And if there are young girls in the house the decorations include pictures, or clay images, of other moon dwellers.

In every courtyard, however humble, the women set up an altar and prepare for the services with great care. Five round plates are arranged and filled with whatever fruit the family can afford — but the shape of each variety of fruit must be round. And in the center are the round moon-cakes baked especially for this holiday, round as the Circle of Happiness. Nearby are the red candles ready to be lighted, and the bundles of incense in the family urn. And from the candleholders and the incense urn hang strings of paper money. Behind the low altar the family places a large paper scroll, upon which is painted the Moon Rabbit sitting under the Sacred Cinnamon Tree, or the three-legged toad entangled in a string of coins.

Exactly at midnight, when the moon shines brightest, and every decorated courtyard, with its candles flickering and incense rising in curls of faint smoke, seems like a tiny fairyland, the family gathers for the brief service to the Queen of the Skies. After the service, the scroll picturing the Moon Rabbit or Moon Toad is burned, so that their souls may return to the moon, where they dwell.

Then each family eats the festival meal out in the moonlight, and celebrates, each according to its means.

The holiday lasts for three days. In the villages people

appear in the streets with masks. Music is heard everywhere. There are lion-dancers and stilt-walkers to amuse the people. The rabbit, who, like the moon, sleeps with his eyes open, and the three-legged toad, who is also a moon

THE MOON RABBIT UNDER THE CINNAMON TREE
After a Chinese jade

dweller, are seen everywhere. The first promises a long life to those who are virtuous; and the second offers wealth for those who please the Moon Queen.

The Man in the Moon

Besides the rabbit and the toad, there also dwells on the moon a very old man with a long gray beard, whose name is Yueh Lao Yeh, the Old Matchmaker. He spends all his days deciding who should be married to whom. For all marriages, so it is believed, are prepared on the T'ai Yin, the Great Female Principle.

The story is told of a certain rich young man who once met a graybeard by the roadside, reading a book in the moonlight.

"What are you reading in this light?" asked the young man.

"I am reading the names of all the future bridegrooms and their brides. And with the red cord of my sleeve I tie the feet of the men to the feet of the maidens they are to marry."

"Can you show me my bride?" asked the young man.

"Indeed, I can," said the Old Matchmaker. "She is the youngest daughter of the poor vegetable vender down this road."

The rich young man went down the road and learned that the vegetable vender had only an infant daughter. And in his heart he decided to prove the prophecy false. He hired a man to kill the infant; then went on his way.

Fourteen years later the rich young man, in a province far from his home, met a young maiden so beautiful that he decided to marry her without delay. After the wedding ceremonies, the happy bridegroom learned from his bride that when she was very young someone tried to kill her, but she was rescued by her father, an old vegetable vender. Then the young man realized that whomsoever the

Moon a great calamity would befall the valley in which he lived.

Huan Ching heeded the warning and went up with his wife and his children to a high place, leaving his herds and other possessions behind him. The calamity predicted by the magician took place as he had foretold and on the day he said that it would happen. Huan Ching's cattle and his house and all he had were destroyed. And all those in the valley who did not heed the warning of the magician lost their lives. But Huan and his family spent the day on the heights celebrating their escape from destruction.

And what better way can one celebrate on a mountain-top than to fly kites?

Ever since then, according to legend, on the ninth day of the Ninth Moon the men and boys go out to fly their kites on the heights.

The girls come out to watch them. And the women prepare a feast for the evening when the men and children return home.

Most of the kites flown on this day are made of paper, but some are made of silk. The kites are designed in various forms and in many gay colors.

Some kites are made in the shape of bats, because the bat is supposed to live for a thousand years and stands for happiness and a long life.

Some kites are made in the shape of butterflies, because the butterfly stands for pleasure and a happy marriage.

Many of them are made in the shape of fish, for nothing

is a better symbol to the Chinese of health, wealth and a big family.

There are also kites in the shape of geese, peacocks, tigers and the tortoise — all of them symbols of good things.

Thousands of people appear on this day on the heights to fly their kites or to watch the flights and the games. Soon the air is filled with red, green and yellow kites, quivering aloft like great flags.

And as soon as the kites are in the air, the people begin a strange and amusing game. Each kiteflier tries to cross the string of another kite; then he begins to pull and vibrate his string in such a way as to cut the string of the opponent's kite.

The great crowd of people watching these games twit the kitefliers; and when a string is cut and a kite is downed, a great shout goes up from the spectators.

Some of the very large kites often carry aloft a lute in which the wind makes music. By pulling the strings of the kite a kiteflier may even succeed in playing a tune. Other kites have firecrackers attached to the bamboo frames which are set to go off after the kites are very high in the air.

It takes great skill to cut an opponent's string, to play a tune on a lute attached to a kite, or to set off firecrackers without injuring the kite. It takes great skill; and it also takes good luck. The men and boys come prepared. Each wears the claw of a tiger to make him brave, or carries an amulet of peachstones to ward off misfortune, or wears on his ankle the nail of a coffin to protect him from an accident. And those who can afford it carry the best charm of all: a jade amulet. Before they release the kites, they rub the amulets in their hands to bring them good luck; and they rub the amulets again when they win. For jade is the stone of the seven virtues: it gleams like Benevolence; it is luminous like Knowledge; it is tough like Uprightness; it is harmless like Power; it is spotless like Purity; it is durable like Eternity; and, like Moral Principles, it does not spoil with frequent use. It is a good charm to have around on the Kiteflying Festival.

Chung Yang Chieh is a festival which the boys in particular eagerly await each year. And it is the happy kind of holiday one would expect to find in China.

III   THE
HINDU
HOLIDAYS

"Nine and Sixty Ways"

Of all the holidays in the world, the holidays of India may be the most difficult for us to understand. And these are the reasons why:

To begin with, India is a land of many religions. India (recently divided into India and Pakistan) is the adopted country of a faith established in Persia over three thousand years ago by the religious leader Zarathustra or Zoroaster. This faith has its own sacred scriptures and is known in India as the Parsi faith or Zoroastrianism.

India is also the home of a religion that calls itself the Faith of the Conquerors, Jainism, and India is the native land of the followers of Guru Nanak, who established the Sikh religion. The Sikhs, who number about three million, are easily recognized by what is known as the Five K's: *Kes* (long hair); *Kunga* (a wooden comb); *Kach* (white drawers); *Kara* (an iron bracelet); and *Kirpan* (a short dagger).

In addition, one in every nine people in India is a Moslem. Most Moslem-Hindus are now in Pakistan.

There are also ten million people in India who are Christians.

The Parsis, the Jains, the Sikhs, the Moslems and the Christians in India all celebrate their own holidays.

But the rest of the people, well over 300 million of them, are the followers of Hinduism, a religion that consists of many sects. And they celebrate the holidays of Hinduism.

The Hindu holidays are so many that there are not enough days in the year to celebrate them separately, so that on certain days several holidays are celebrated together. They have two-in-one, three-in-one and even five-in-one holidays.

Certain festivities are celebrated in some parts of India which are practically unknown in other parts of the country.

Some holidays are for men only; others, for women only.

The same holidays are often celebrated in different parts of India, but for different reasons.

Again, some holidays are in honor of certain gods (of which there are millions in India); and quite different holidays are kept in honor of the same gods known by different names.

The same holidays are sometimes celebrated in different parts of India on different days, due to the way the Hindus count their days and months; and because two different eras are used in their calendar: one beginning with 57 B.C. and another with A.D. 78.

As if all this were not confusing enough, there are also fasts and feasts which are kept only for a given number of years, after which they are no longer observed. (There is, for instance, a woman's holiday, called Rishi Panchami, the Festival of the Great Bear, which is observed by Hindu women for seven successive years. After seven years they no longer observe this festival.)

No wonder the stranger finds the holidays of India a puzzling maze. But as he studies the holidays carefully, the confusion lifts slowly like a fog under a bright sun. Then he sees that all the Hindu holidays are of three kinds:

1. FESTIVITIES IN HONOR OF THE SUN, THE MOON AND THE STARS. The Hindus, like all the early nations of mankind, were nature worshipers at first, and the worship of the heavenly bodies still plays an important part in their religion and their lives.

2. FESTIVITIES IN HONOR OF THE GODS. The Hindus believe in Trimurti, the Three-in-One-God. Trimurti consists of: Brahma, the Creator; Vishnu, the Preserver; and Siva, the Destroyer. But these gods have multiplied until there are now millions of gods. In the Hindu religion, all

the gods are manifestations of One God. But in the ritual and holidays each manifestation is treated as a distinct and separate divinity.

3. HOLIDAYS IN HONOR OF SPIRITS, ANIMALS AND PLANTS. In India the cow, the monkey and the snake are considered sacred; as are the banyan tree, the coconut, the elephant apple and other trees, fruits and grasses. Some of these animals and plants are commemorated in the holidays. The monkey Hanuman is considered one of the Seven Immortals, and his birthday is observed by many Hindu sects.

Most of the holidays are celebrated differently by different sects of India; and each sect may have a different ritual as well as a different explanation of the holidays.

How is one to know which is right?

The answer to that question is easy. They are all right.

There are nine and sixty ways of constructing tribal lays,
And every single one of them is right!

And that goes for the Hindu holidays.

The holidays and the beliefs related to the holidays reflect the folklore and the ritual of the Hindus, rather than their great religion.

(Of course, the holidays and the ritual are not in the least confusing to the Hindus. That is because they know their own religion and the sacred books upon which their holidays are founded. But the Hindu scriptures are little known to the people of the West, and therefore they find the Hindu holidays more difficult to understand.)

A Not-so-happy New Year's Day

All the people on earth celebrate the new year. They do not celebrate it on the same day, nor for the same reason. Yet the New Year's Days of the different nations all come at the beginning of a season.

Just as the people of long ago found it hard to decide when the day begins, whether at sunrise or sunset, at midnight or midnoon, so too they found it hard to decide which of the four seasons ushers in the new year.

The Hindus solved the problem very neatly: they celebrate the beginning of each of the four seasons.

The beginning of summer is celebrated with Ratha Yathra and the transfer of the Lord Vishnu from his winter to his summer home.

The autumn is started in many parts with a holiday called Diwali, which is the New Year of Business.

Winter arrives with a New Year's festival of great importance, for the sun then enters the sign in the zodiac which we call the House of Capricorn, the Goat. The Hindu astronomers call this zodiac sign Makara, the Alligator. And the holiday is called Makara Sankranti.

Then comes spring, the favorite season of all the nations on earth, when the sun enters the House of Aries, the Ram. And about the time we celebrate Easter, the Hindus celebrate their New Year's Day proper, called Dhvajaropana and also known as Guddhi Padava.

The House of the Alligator

Every year, near the middle of January, the Hindus celebrate the passing of the winter solstice, when the sun is on its way south again through the House of Makara, the Alligator.

Makara Sankranti is a great bathing festival. On this day, practically everyone in India wishes he could bathe in the Ganges, most sacred of the rivers. And the most sacred spot is where the Ganges and the Jumna rivers meet, at the city of Allahabad, the City of God.

BATHERS IN THE HOLY WATER
OF THE GANGES

The very orthodox Hindus will make the pilgrimage to that city, even if they have to face hunger and cold, accident and disease, to be there for the bathing on Makara Sankranti or the month of the Holy Fair at Allahabad. In some years as many as a million people arrive in this city of the north to have their sins washed away in the Ganges on the Holiday of the Alligator.

Those who cannot reach the Ganges bathe in other rivers or streams. For bathing is part of this great holiday. This is also a holiday for family reunions, almsgiving, the opening of great religious fairs, and for remembering the family priest with a present.

In some parts of India, on this holiday, women who want to have children take coconuts and secretly leave them in a Brahman home. Or they bring gifts of betel nuts and spices to Brahman wives. Or they take coconuts to their neighbors and beg for an exchange of fruit, saying: "Take a toy and give a child."

This act they believe will fulfill their wish.

During this holiday every member of the family, and all guests who come to visit, are served sugared sesamum seed, with the greeting: "Eat sweetly, speak sweetly."

And this intended to banish all quarreling for the year.

Dhvajaropana

Three months after the Makara Sankranti comes the New Year's Day proper. But in no way does it resemble celebrations of the new year that are held anywhere else in the world.

An important part of this holiday consists of prayers to Sitala, goddess of smallpox. And the people eat leaves of the neem tree, a tree sacred to all the disease goddesses.

New Year's Day, such a merry holiday for most people in the world, is really a sad observance for the Hindus, who must think all day of Sitala, goddess of smallpox, cholera and bubonic plague.

For centuries India has been afflicted with these three plagues. With the arrival of the hot summer months comes also the dread of another epidemic. So the Hindus worship Sitala with prayers and offerings, asking her to prevent the sickness.

Sitala is represented by an image with a pale-yellow face, clothed in blood-red garments. In one hand she carries a bundle of reeds; and with the other she holds the reins of her ass, the despised beast upon which she travels everywhere.

The offerings made to Sitala consist of betel leaves, red flowers, some cooked foods. Sitala loves everything red, and beside her shrine, usually in the shade of a neem tree, there rises the tall bamboo bearing a blood-red banner to mark the spot. There the people come with gifts. Most of the worshipers are mothers, who fear disease for the children more than for themselves. They send up supplications to the goddess of smallpox; and they plead with her, calling her *Mata,* meaning "Mother." For although she is the goddess of plague, she is nevertheless divine and must be worshiped with reverence.

Then, too, if they succeed in pleasing Sitala with their prayers and offerings she may take pity on them and keep away from their doors.

The Holiday of Incarnations (Krishnavatara)

The Three Keys

There are three keys to the Hindu religion which also fit their holidays. The names of these keys are: *Karma*, *Avatar* and *Trimurti*.

1. *Karma* is the eternal law of life. This law asserts: "From good must come good, and from evil must come evil."

But the reward of good and the punishment of evil do not take place as soon as the thought enters the mind, or the word leaves the mouth or the deed is done. Rewards and punishments are usually made in the next incarnation.

2. *Avatar* means the incarnation of a god in human form; or the new form a soul of any living thing takes after leaving its old form or body.

Nobody ever dies, according to this belief. When the deathless soul leaves the body of any living creature it is reincarnated into another body. It goes through an *Avatar*. The souls of all the living things on earth go through a continuous cycle of changing bodies. This is known as the transmigration of souls.

That is when the law of life, *Karma*, is carried out. When a good man dies he is rewarded by being reborn, or reincarnated, into a better state. But if a soul is evil, then it is reincarnated into a worse state.

3. *Trimurti* really means "Three shapes" and is the name of the Three-in-One God, or the Triad, or what is sometimes called the Hindu Trinity. The three gods are: Brahma, the Creator; Vishnu, the Preserver; and Siva, the Destroyer.

The Trimurti rules the universe.

For hundreds of thousands of years these gods married and had children, and their wives and children became gods, each ruling over a special domain of the world. The children, in turn, married and had children, and the number of gods multiplied, until there are millions of gods in India today.

Even in the earliest days of the Hindu religion, known as the Vedic Age or the Age of the Vedas, we already find gods and spirits for practically everything under the sun. There is a sun god, a rain god, a fire god, a dawn goddess, a wind spirit, a sky father, an earth mother, and so on. And since the Vedic Age these gods have greatly multiplied.

Not only do the gods have families, but they also appear in human or animal form to perform great deeds in the world.

And many years ago, every time a god went through another incarnation, it became the occasion for another Hindu holiday.

The Incarnations of Vishnu (Janmashtami)

There are a number of important festivals in India devoted to Vishnu, the Preserver.

Vishnu, so it is believed, has gone through many incarnations. Every time the demons threatened to destroy the world, Vishnu assumes a human or animal form and saved the earth and its inhabitants. Each event is remembered with a holiday in Vishnu's honor.

In the first three incarnations Vishnu appeared as a fish, a tortoise and a boar to save the earth from a deluge which threatened to drown all living things and permanently cover the earth with water.

Later Vishnu appeared as a man-lion, as a dwarf, as the son of a great sage, and as a prince. And in each incarnation he performed deeds that are commemorated.

Vishnu's most memorable incarnation was his eighth, when he appeared as Krishna, son of Prince Vasudeva and Princess Devaki. The miracles that attended Krishna's birth and childhood, the heroic deeds he performed when he grew up, and how he died of a wound in the heel inflicted by an arrow, are described in the greatest of all Hindu sacred epics, the Mahabharata, an ancient Hindu epic of 110,000 stanzas.

Krishna's birth is celebrated during the summer throughout India by all sects and all castes. In the homes a space is
cleared to represent the birth-room, in which the image
of the baby Krishna, cast in gold, brass or plaster, is surrounded by all the other personages in his eventful infancy.
Sometimes the infant is placed in a swinging cradle and
decorated with garlands of fragrant flowers. In the temples
a great ceremony is conducted as for the birth of a noble
son. Mantras, which are similar to our Psalms, are sung at
midnight. There is music and dancing. Children are given
sweets. And since Krishna as a child was very fond of milk,
many varieties of dairy dishes are prepared on this holiday.

The Pilgrimage to Puri

In addition to celebrating his birthday, the Hindus remember Krishna in an annual pilgrimage to Puri, a town
on the Bay of Bengal, which is also known as Jagannath or
Juggernaut.

Puri is a holy city full of temples, with the most important devoted to Krishna, who is also called Juggernaut, and
to his brother and sister, Balabhadra and Subhadra. In
this temple are kept the three chariots belonging to Juggernaut and his brother and sister. Juggernaut's chariot, the
biggest of them all, is as high as a three-story building and
so long that it is mounted on sixteen immense wheels.

Once every year, toward the end of June, thousands of

Hindus gather in Puri to take part in the Procession of the Chariots.

On the day of the celebration, early in the morning, one hundred and eight pitchers of water are drawn from a well reserved for the ceremonies, and the images of Juggernaut and his brother and sister are washed with great reverence, then placed in their respective chariots. The huge and ornate vehicles are then dragged by the people from the temple where they had remained all winter, to a summer home, one and a half miles away.

Those who make the pilgrimage to Puri believe that infinite good is to be derived from the sight of Juggernaut in his chariot. And they consider it a great honor to take part in dragging the enormous chariots for at least a little distance.

There was a time when some of the worshipers on this occasion threw themselves under the immense wheels of the Juggernaut chariot when it was in motion, to attain a holy death. This practice has been forbidden. But the people still come to Puri in hundreds of thousands each year to take part in the Procession of the Chariots, and in the feast that follows the procession.

Those who cannot make the pilgrimage to Puri go to the nearest Juggernaut temple where the Procession of the Chariots is re-enacted, and they take part in that procession. But they do not consider it as beneficient as taking part in the Chariot Festival in Puri.

The Festival of the Divine Mother (Durga Puja)

In the autumn, toward the end of September or early in October, comes a ten-day holiday which is celebrated in India, chiefly in Bengal, and with greater religious fervor and ceremonial pomp than any other in that land. It is called Durga Puja, the Festival of the Divine Mother.

Durga is placed above all other goddesses of India.

Durga is the wife of Siva, the Destroyer, one of the Hindu Trinity. She is also the mother of two daughters and two sons who have attained great distinction among the gods.

One of her daughters is Saraswati, who married Brahma, the Creator, first in the Hindu Trinity. Saraswati then became the goddess of the Nine Muses. She is often called the Hindu Minerva.

) Durga's second daughter, Lakshmi, married Vishnu, the Preserver — second in the Hindu Trinity — and Lakshmi became the goddess of wealth and beauty.

Ganesha, Durga's elephant-headed son, the god of wisdom and the bestower of success, is so loved in India that books in that land begin with: "I bow to Ganesha!" And many holidays are dedicated to this god.

Durga's second son, Karttikeya, who rides on a peacock

as the commander in chief of the army of the gods, is the god of war.

No wonder Durga, the Divine Mother, is held in such reverence!

Durga is only one of the names by which the Divine Mother of the Divine Children, and the wife of the Auspicious Destroyer, is known. Durga has a thousand names; and under each name she has a different power.

In the temples and in the homes Durga appears in the image of a very tall woman, whose fair skin is tinged with the sacred color, yellow. She has ten arms, and in each arm carries a weapon with which to destroy evil. And she rides on the sacred lion.

On the holiday dedicated to her, Durga is represented as trampling underfoot the demon Mahishaur, who terrorized the earth until he was slain by the Divine Mother. During this holiday her image, which appears everywhere, is surrounded by images of her sons and daughters. And upon Durga's head rests a crown, sparkling with jewels or beads of various colors.

Before the holiday arrives the markets are full of images of Durga made of clay, or wood, or other inexpensive materials, and ranging in size from a few inches to images ten or even twenty feet in height. Everyone buys an image according to his means, the way people buy Christmas trees in other lands. But no home, however humble, goes without its image of Durga on this holiday.

On this autumn festival it is proper to bring as offerings

to the Divine Mother, the Force of the Universe, every product of the earth — animal, mineral and vegetable. In some parts of India sacrifices of black male goats are made

DURGA AND HER LION

Slaying the demon Mahishaur, who is giving up his buffalo form. Ganesha and his rat are here, and Saraswati, Lakshmi and Karttikeya with his peacock. Illustration is based on a popular picture

to Durga. In other parts gourds or other vegetables are sliced with a sword in the presence of the goddess, in remembrance of her slaying of the demon Mahishaur.

The Moment of Worship

Puja means "worship." And the time to worship Durga and to offer her the sacrifices is set with great precision. The exact time when the spirit of the Divine Mother lights upon her image in the homes or in the temples is determined each year by the astronomers, down to the last second. It is believed that her appearance in spirit lasts only exactly as long "as a mustard seed can stand on the pointed edge of a cow's horn." And in that moment the sacrifice and service to Durga must begin.

The worshipers surround the altar and pray for the spirit to take possession of the image. During the services, the readings and the prayers from the sacred texts must be done without flaw or error. Omitting a word or even a syllable can lead to great catastrophe. That is why two people are always chosen to recite the prescribed prayers. One reads and the other listens carefully. If the reader stumbles over a word or omits a syllable, the second reader, usually a priest, instantly corrects the mistake, so that it sounds as if no mistake had occurred. And evil is warded off.

For each of the ten days there exists a prescribed ritual.

Most of the time is given to celebrating. It is customary to visit friends who may have been neglected during the year. This is the time to remember with letters friends and relatives who live in distant places.

Durga Puja is also the time for children to honor their mothers, as we do on Mother's Day, with gifts and greetings. It is a ten-day-long Mother's Day.

For nine days the image of Durga is worshiped. And on the tenth day her image, and the images of her daughters and sons, and all the lesser gods that surround them on this holiday, are taken out of the homes and temples. They are carried through the streets by young men in a grave procession, followed by older worshipers and bands of musicians. The procession always ends near a river bank. There the images are placed reverently on a boat that is rowed out to midstream. And there the images are stripped of their silk clothes and valuable ornaments. Then the images are thrown into water deep enough to submerge them. And everybody watching the ceremony shouts: "Victory to the Divine Mother! Victory to Durga!"

After this ceremony the people return to their homes and spend the rest of the day in feasting and entertaining guests who arrive in streams to wish, and to be wished, good luck and happiness.

The Victories of Rama (Dussera)

During the ten-day Festival of the Divine Mother a pageant is presented in every city, town or village throughout northern India, much as the pageant of the birth of Jesus is presented in schools and churches before Christmas. The pageant in India is presented for two hours each day on ten successive days.

The pageant is not about the Goddess Durga and how she killed the buffalo-headed demon. The pageant, in fact, has nothing to do with any events in the life of Durga, or her husband, or her children. It is, instead, about the victories of Rama, or Ramachandra, son of King Dasáratha, who lived a million and three hundred thousand years ago.

The annual pageant is called Ram Lila. And it is based upon the famous and sacred Hindu epic Ramayana, which consists of 24,000 stanzas.

The Ram Lila presents certain dramatic incidents of the great epic, which are as well known to the Hindus and their children as the miracles at the birth of Jesus or the Flight to Egypt are known to us.

Every year the people throughout India gather in the market places, which are cleared for the occasion, and they watch the Rama Lila with excitement and interest as if they were seeing it for the first time. And there is great rivalry between neighboring towns and villages as to who will put on the pageant with greater pomp, a richer display of costumes and better music.

The story of this pageant is very involved and concerns, mainly, the events in the wars between Rama (who was really the seventh incarnation of the Lord Vishnu, the Preserver) and Ravana, the cruel demon with ten faces and twenty hands who threatened to conquer the earth below and the gods in heaven.

BURNING THE EFFIGY OF RAVANA

Rama's forces were under the command of the great General Hanuman, who was a monkey, and Hanuman led his forces to great victories over the enemies of mankind and the gods. The most exciting parts of the pageant are those dealing with the battle scenes in which Hanuman, dressed in a glorious costume, his long tail standing up erect behind his head, rushes in without fear of danger, leading his men to victory over the enemy.

In between battle scenes, a chorus sings parts from the great epic Ramayana; and people respond to given passages with a great shout of: "Victory to Rama! Death to Ravana!"

The ten-day pageant ends with the death of Ravana, who is burned in effigy. The image of the dead demon, made of bamboo and colored paper, is placed on a platform and blown up with fireworks.

And the excited audience shouts and the people stamp their feet, as the victory is celebrated of Rama over Ravana, of good over evil.

The Festival of the Garland of Lights
(Diwali or Dipavali)

Some holidays in India are just for mothers, others are for brothers and their sisters; or for farmers; or for priests; or for the worshipers of Siva. And there is one very important holiday which is meant for merchants, though it is celebrated by everybody. It is called Diwali (short for Dipavali) meaning "the garland of lights."

Diwali comes toward the end of October or the beginning of November and is actually five holidays, one following the other. Each of the five holidays has its own name; and none has anything in common with the others, except that they arrive five days in a row.

The first of these holidays, Dhana Trayodashi, is the New Year of Business.

The second holiday commemorates the triumph of the great god Vishnu over the very evil demon Narakarasura.

The third day is given to the worship of Lakshmi, Vishnu's wife, the goddess of wealth and beauty.

The fourth day is called Bali Worship Day, and is considered the Dipavali proper. This day commemorates a very ancient battle between the castes. On this day, also, cows and bullocks are washed, fed, adorned with garlands of flowers, and paraded through the streets. When the sacred animals are returned home they are welcomed with lighted lanterns which are waved about them to ward off evil.

The last day, the Yama holiday, is devoted to brothers and sisters. Every boy or man is expected to eat the feast of this day with his sister. And, if he has none, he goes to a cousin. And he presents to his sister or cousin the most expensive gift he can afford.

In some parts of India the first day of this holiday is

most important; in some the fourth; and in some all five
are celebrated equally with great rejoicing.

Rakhi Bandhana

Another brother-sister custom, similar to the Yama
celebration, is the widespread Hindu custom best known
as Rakhi Bandhana, or Rakhi Purnima, although it has
many other names.

During the full moon of the month of Sravan, toward
the end of July, sisters bind their brothers' wrists with
rakhi, or amulets consisting of silk threads, or silver or gold
wires. The wealthy use *rakhi* of coral, strings of pearls, and
even precious jewels. The amulets are supposed to protect
the brothers from evil during the ensuing year, and pledge
them to protect their sisters in time of need.

The custom is based on legendary events in Indian history when men and gods were under Bali's tyranny.

In some parts of India, in addition to sisters observing
Rakhi Bandhana, mothers and wives too bind sons and
husbands with amulets. And when the *rakhi* is tied on, they
say:

"With the bond by which the great, strong, demon-king
Bali was bound, I bind you. O, amulet! Do not fall off!"

The Silver Is Red

For days before the arrival of Diwali, the five-in-one
holiday, great preparations are made for it throughout

India. Shops and homes are scoured, walls are painted or whitewashed, windows are made to sparkle, and the doorways are decorated with garlands of flowers. Before each door, on the ground or on the floor, there is skillfully painted with white flour a design that is certain to bring good luck.

GOOD LUCK DESIGN, *ALIPANA*
Painted on the ground at Diwali

The merchants settle their accounts with their customers, like the Chinese before New Year's Day. Then the merchants close their books for the year, and they gather their silver coins in a pile. Before this pile of coins they say a prayer to Lakshmi, goddess of wealth and good fortune.

Then they do a very strange thing: they smear the coins

with powdered yellow turmeric and with red lead. This is done to make the silver coins resemble gold. For Lakshmi, one of the most important of Hindu deities and wife of Vishnu, the Preserver, is not represented by an image but by a gold coin. And for months after the holidays the coins circulating in India are stained.

Those who have a gold coin treat it as if it were the image of their goddess of good fortune. They bathe the coin in sacred water or in milk, which is sacred in India; and they pray to it. But since the poor may not have gold coins on this holiday, they worship the silver coins which have been stained with yellow and red, and pray for luck during the New Year of Business.

Schools close the day before Diwali. And boys and girls are busy during the entire day pouring oil into tiny earthenware bowls and cutting cords into short wicks. Hundreds of these little lamps are prepared and set out in rows along the parapets of the flat-roofed houses. A well-to-do family might have as many as a thousand of these little oil lamps. In recent times in some places garlands of multicolored electric lights are used instead.

On the first night of this holiday all the little lamps are lighted, and every house is outlined with borders of flickering lights. As night falls, the towns and the cities suddenly appear festive and unreal as in a golden dream.

The lights on the roofs and the many lamps in the houses are all kept bright throughout Diwali, for this is the time Lakshmi, goddess of wealth, comes on the wings of the

Heavenly Owl to visit the dwellers on earth and to bless them. And the people want to make sure that her way to their homes is well lighted.

Diwali, like practically every holiday in India, begins with bathing. People arise very early and rub their bodies with perfumed oil. Then all the members of the family, from the infant to the grandfather, must have a perfumed bath. They dress in their finest clothes, for it is customary to wear new things on Diwali. Even the poorest people try to have at least one new garment to put on, for good luck.

After they are dressed, they eat. Most holidays in India begin with fasting and end with feasting, but on Diwali breakfast is eaten. And at noon fourteen different dishes are served, or a dish made of fourteen different kinds of food. And the evening meal is brightened with fourteen lamps. This number is in honor of the moon, which changes faces every fourteen days.

For while Diwali is the holiday celebrating the Business New Year and honoring Lakshmi, the goddess of wealth, it is also a holiday honoring the moon, and a time when the sacred cows and bullocks are worshiped.

During Diwali visits are made to the temples of the various gods, games re-enacting historic events are played; visits are paid to relatives and friends; and everybody bathes often, and at least once in a flowing river. For although all water is considered sacred in India, the water of a flowing river has great power to wash all sins away.

DIWALI
A house adorned with lamps

Naraka Chaturdashi

Many beautiful legends are told about the origin of the Diwali celebrations; and the most fascinating is told on the second day of this holiday, called Naraka Chaturdashi.

There was a terrible demon, long ago, whose name was Narakarasura. And every time the demon saw a beautiful maiden he carried her off to his domain and there he kept her prisoner. This went on until Narakarasura had sixteen thousand unhappy captives. And still the demon was not satisfied. He began to cast his eyes on princesses and even on the daughters of the gods. And once he went so far as to steal the earrings of Aditi, mother of Vishnu, Indra, and ten other gods.

By this time the women of heaven and earth were aroused. They came before Vishnu, the Creator, pleading with him to destroy Narakarasura.

Unfortunately, though Narakarasura was such an evil demon when it came to women, he was pious and virtuous in every other respect. In fact, his piety and various good deeds had earned so much spiritual worth for him in the eyes of the gods that no one, not even Vishnu, could do him any harm.

Vishnu had to wait patiently until the demon's evil deeds outweighed his good deeds. Only then could he send his hosts to destroy the kidnaper. But when the demon was finally surrounded in his stronghold by Vishnu's messengers and they were ready to put him to death, Narakarasura pleaded:

"From good must come good, and from evil must come evil!"

"That we believe," said Vishnu's messengers.

"The worth of a good deed done can never be wiped out," said Narakarasura.

"That too we believe," replied Vishnu's messengers.

"Then by virtue of all the good deeds I have done, I ask that at this hour of death I be granted one wish by the Lord Vishnu."

"What is your wish?" asked Vishnu.

"I wish that the day of my death be remembered with feasting during the Holiday of Lights."

His wish was granted; and his head was severed; and all the sixteen thousand maidens were freed from the demon's stronghold.

On the second day of Diwali, the story of Narakarasura, which sends chills down the backs of young girls, is told much as it is written down in the sacred book Kalika Purana, embellished with details added by the storyteller.

The people rejoice, as Narakarasura wished, but they rejoice that Vishnu slew the demon and freed the world from this monster.

(The celebration of a victory over an evil spirit or an evil man or an evil enemy is to be found among all religious and national holidays of the world.)

The Festival of Tools (Visvakarma Puja)

There are many patron gods and goddesses in India. Some of them are very good, and people celebrate on certain days each year to thank them for the many blessings they have brought. But some of the patron gods and goddesses are evil, and people try to placate them with prayers and gifts, intended to ward off their wrath.

There is the good goddess Gauri, giver of harvests and protector of women, who is honored with a festival each year by the women of the highest Hindu caste. There is, on the other hand, the festival dedicated to the evil goddess Shashthi and the black cat, who must be treated with respect and worshiped by mothers in a special holiday each year to prevent evil befalling their children.

The most unusual holiday in the world is the one dedicated in India to Visvakarma, the patron god of all artisans.

On this holiday, which arrives at the end of the sixth month of the Hindu year, in every home and in every shop a pitcher is set in a place of honor, or in a niche reserved for family worship. This pitcher represents the god Visvakarma.

Before this pitcher the people place the most important tool in their work or in their trade. Boys and girls place there the schoolbook they use most. Musicians place the instruments they play. Artists put their favorite brushes before the pitcher; writers, their pens and ink; tailors, their scissors; seamstresses, their thread and needles, shoemakers, their awls; gardeners, their rakes; fishermen, their nets; and so on. Each, according to his craft or activity, places his most important tool beside the pitcher representing the patron god of all useful tools.

Even the housewife comes and places her favorite broom in the place of honor.

Then each artisan and craftsman, artist and student, housewife and laborer lights a candle in front of the pitcher and his or her tool. They bow before the tool, the pitcher and the lighted candle, and pray silently. They thank their tools for all the help given them in the past; and implore them to do their utmost for their owners in the coming year. It is a prayer of both thankfulness and supplication.

After the prayer, some place flowers on their honored tools; some burn incense before them; and some sprinkle them with scented water.

After the simple ceremonies at home, people gather in parks or public places, and the day is spent in games and in feasting. No one goes to work. It is a workers' holiday, similar to our Labor Day. Yet it is unlike our Labor Day. Our Labor Day was first celebrated in 1882, whereas the Festival of Tools is many centuries old; Labor Day is secular, whereas the Festival of Tools is a religious celebration; and whereas Labor Day is dedicated to the worker, the Festival of Tools is dedicated to the instrument the worker uses in his work.

Holi (The Fire Festival)

On the fifteenth day of the Light Half of the Moon, in the Hindu month of Phalguna, the people of India celebrate the gayest of all their holidays, called Holi.

Holi, which occurs sometime in March, is clearly a spring festival.

It is *the* spring festival, although there is another spring holiday that is celebrated some three weeks earlier, which is known as Basanta Panchami, shortened to Basanta.

The Poet's Spring

Basanta, which in Sanskrit means "yellow" — the sacred color of India — is the symbol of spring. On this holiday young men wear yellow turbans and scarfs. And practically everybody, young and old, wears something green to honor the garment of the green earth during this season.

Spring has been the favorite topic of poets the world over. And the great Hindu poets of ancient days were no exception. They devoted many of their songs to Basanta, and in some way they connected the arrival of spring with Saraswati, Brahma's wife, and the goddess of the sixty-four arts and sciences.

Of all the Hindu gods and goddesses, Saraswati appeals

most to poets. Though her husband, Brahma, is represented as having four faces, and her mother, Durga, as having ten arms, there is nothing superhuman about Saraswati. Yet she looks most like a goddess. She is represented as a beautiful girl, snow-white in complexion, sitting serenely on a white lotus that floats in crystal-clear water, or riding on her famous swan. Everything about her is white — her skin, her flowers, her swan-carriage, her clothes. In one hand she holds a book, since she is the goddess of letters; and in the other she holds a harp, since she is also the goddess of music.

When Saraswati is worshiped on Basanta, the offerings made to her are white mango bloom, or any white flowers, and sweets from a white herb called sesamum. For everything white honors Saraswati; and everything black offends her.

On Basanta everyone, from the oldest to the youngest member of the family, fasts until noon. Before noon the family gathers around a clay image of Saraswati. If they have no clay image they use a brass or copper urn filled with clear water. Before the image or the urn they place some books, writing materials (but not ink), musical instruments, or anything representing the arts and the sciences, provided it is not black.

When all is in order, the head of the family leads the prescribed prayers, which are chanted by all of them.

If there is a boy in the house five years old, he is introduced to learning at this time. If for any reason the child cannot be taught at this time, he is not introduced to learning until two years later. For even numbers are considered unlucky in India, and he could not be taught when six years of age. The father, or a priest, or a teacher recites the Sanskrit alphabet, and the boy repeats the fifty letters as they are given to him.

"A," says the teacher.

"A," repeats the boy.

"Ba," says the teacher.

"Ba," repeats the boy.

And so on all the way down to the last letter.

Then the boy is given a piece of chalk and his hand is guided in tracing the first Sanskrit letter before the image of Saraswati.

The ritual finished, the family breaks the fast. And the rest of the day is devoted to games, concerts, or any other entertainment. The pleasant Basanta is over.

But the *real* spring holiday is actually still three weeks away.

The Bonfires of Holi

How it all started nobody really knows. But for a week before Holi boys everywhere in India, in city neighborhoods, in towns and in villages, go from door to door collecting fuel for a bonfire. No one ever turns them away, for it is considered a duty to contribute some fuel, or money for fuel, for the Holi Fire Festival. And if some boys filch a little wood from a woodpile, or pilfer shavings from a carpenter's shop, or carry off a broken piece of furniture at this time of the year, the owners do not even complain.

The wood, the papers, the old furniture, staves of discarded barrels, old crates, torn straw or bamboo baskets, and anything else that will burn, are stacked up neatly into a huge pile and made ready for the night of Holi.

When the moon is high and bright in the sky, the bonfires are lighted all over India, with great shouts of joy and the blowing of horns and the beating of drums. Once lighted, each bonfire becomes sacred and an object of worship. The crowds, mostly men and boys, walk reverently around the fire. But as the night progresses, the merriment rises and grows boisterous. The people dance their favorite folk dances around the fire. And, as they dance, they sing the songs meant especially for this night, which relate in great detail their god Krishna's adventures as a young man with the merry milkmaids of Brindaban. The events and the language of these songs make the young girls blush. And that makes the men laugh.

At sunrise water is poured on the embers to put the fires out. Then everyone dips his fingers into the warm ashes and marks his or her forehead, to bring luck for the coming year. And during the entire day of Holi the people go about with the ash marks on their foreheads.

The day, like the night preceding, is given over to fun and mischief. Boys roam the streets with bamboo blowpipes. And they shower every passerby with liquid or powdered colors. The girls scream in mock horror. Actually they enjoy it, since it is Holi.

FOLK DANCE DURING HOLI

There are many legends to explain the bonfires, the "playing with colors," the blowing of horns and the beating of drums on this holiday.

One legend tells of a time long ago, when a female demon, an ogress named Holika, came down each spring to devour the young children of the villages. When Holika arrived, all the people tried to hide from her. But the ogress sought them out, one by one, and snatched their young children away from them.

Then one year all the people of the villages gathered together and waited for Holika. When she arrived they surrounded her with horns in one hand and fagots in the other. They mocked her and shouted curses and blew their horns so loud that they confused and frightened the wicked ogress. She tried to run away. But there was no place for her to run. She was ringed about by the crowds, who had piled their fagots up about her like a pyre, and they set fire to it. Holika was burned in the great bonfire and never returned to bother them again.

Every spring since then the people celebrate the destruction of the ogress Holika with huge bonfires and mocking songs and the blowing of horns and the beating of drums.

The children of India, if asked which holiday they like best, would undoubtedly choose Holi. Not only the bonfires and spraying colors and singing songs are so much fun, but also eating all day long. For even the poorest people prepare their best food for this day. They serve many delicious dairy dishes, and as many sweets as they can afford, to guests and children.

Holi is as exciting to the children of India as Halloween is to the children of the West.

In different parts of India this holiday is known under different names. In some places it is called the Swing Festival, because they place images of their gods on swings and swing them. And the celebration lasts for three days in some places, and in others for ten. But everywhere it is gay and full of fun for young and old.

Lucky and Unlucky Days

In addition to the many holidays, the Hindus recognize lucky and unlucky seasons, lucky and unlucky days.

All the nations of the earth consider certain times or days in the year especially auspicious or inauspicious. But for the Hindu every day is either lucky or unlucky. Even the hours of the day must be watched with concern.

THE SEASONS. The entire rainy season, which lasts for four months in India, is considered unlucky. And so also is the season from the summer solstice to the winter solstice. But from the winter to the summer solstice is generally a lucky season; and so are all the twelve days, called the *sankranti* days, when the sun crosses from one zodiac sign to another.

THE MONTHS. All the months are divided by the Hindus into two periods of the moon: the Light Moon, from the new to the full moon; and the Dark Moon, from the full to the new moon. The Light Moon is lucky; and the Dark Moon is unlucky.

THE DAYS. The days under the rule of the moon (Monday), Mercury (Wednesday), Jupiter (Thursday) and Venus (Friday) are lucky days. And Monday is the luckiest of them all. But the days under the rule of the sun (Sunday), Mars (Tuesday) and Saturn (Saturday) are unlucky. And the unluckiest day is Saturday.

This sounds much simpler than it really is. For a lucky day may become unlucky, or an unlucky day may become lucky, depending on the position of the planets in relation to each other.

That is why, when a child is born in India, the family priest or an astrologer is asked to set down the position of the stars on a horoscope. Later, when the child is grown and ready to marry, the parents compare the horoscopes of the boy and the girl to see whether they match. If they do not match according to the stars, the wedding is forbidden.

This sometimes leads to polite deception. For when the parents of a boy approach the parents of a girl with a proposal of marriage, these may ask for his horoscope. If they wish to reject him, they just send back the message that the boy's horoscope was matched with that of their daughter's and, alas, the stars did not foretell a happy marriage, or a fruitful one.

Of course, such deception would never be practiced by a truly religious Hindu. He would fear to offend the stars.

For he believes that everything depends upon the stars — the gods, and the sacred animals and plants. This is true not only of his present life, but of the life of his soul during its many, many incarnations.

The Hindus are not alone in their belief in lucky and unlucky days. All the nations on earth consider some days lucky and others unlucky.

We have an old belief that the day on which a child is born determines its character and its future. This belief is expressed in an old verse:

> Monday's child is fair of face,
> Tuesday's child is full of grace,
> Wednesday's child is full of woe,
> Thursday's child has far to go,
> Friday's child is loving and giving,
> Saturday's child works hard for its living,
> And a child that's born on the Sabbath day
> Is fair and wise and good and gay.

IV THE JEWISH HOLIDAYS

The Gift of God (The Sabbath)

In the earliest days of their history, in the days of the patriarchs Abraham, Isaac and Jacob, the Jews were shepherds who wandered in search of green pastures for their flocks. Like all nomads of those early days, they observed the sun, the moon and the stars. From the number of the planets they arrived at the number of the days in a week; from the moon they arrived at a month of 29½ days; and from the sun they calculated that the year has 365 days.

To keep the moon-month in step with the sun-year, the Jews found it necessary to add a full month to every two or three years (as we add one day to every fourth year, which is called the leap year). By adding seven leap-year months to every nineteen years they kept the record straight.

Because the Jewish calendar runs in nineteen-year cycles, their holiday dates, like those of the Chinese, keep shifting back and forth every two or three years.

Some Jewish holidays are very, very old. And the oldest of them all dates back to the days of Abraham. This is also the most sacred of all their holidays. And it arrives not once each year but once every week.

It is the Sabbath, the day of peace and rest.

Since the Jews measure the day from sunset to sunset, their Sabbath arrives on Friday evening, with the appearance of the first star in the skies.

"Remember the Sabbath Day—"

The Sabbath alone of all the holidays is prescribed in the Ten Commandments. The Fourth Commandment reads, in part:

> Remember the sabbath day, to keep it holy.
> Six days shalt thou labor, and do all thy work:
> But the seventh day is the sabbath of the Lord thy God: in it thou shalt not do any work, thou, nor thy son, nor thy daughter, thy manservant, nor thy maidservant, nor thy cattle, nor thy stranger that is within thy gates.

Before this Commandment was set down, no nation on earth recognized a weekly day of rest. People worked day

in, day out, all through the year. The shepherds watching
their flocks, the farmers at their work in the valleys, the
potters at their wheels and the maidservants in the homes,
all worked every day, without a day of rest.

Then the Jews, who had been slaves in Egypt, threw off
their yoke of slavery. And Moses, who led them to freedom, commanded them to work six days each week and
rest on the seventh. This Commandment was intended not
only for the people who accepted the Law, but for all
the people who labored on earth.

Welcome the Bride

Devout Jews welcome the arrival of this weekly holiday in the synagogues by chanting to each other:

"Come, my friend, let us welcome the Bride Sabbath!"

And after the services they return home to begin celebrating the day of rest with the blessing of the wine,
the Kiddush, which commemorates two great events: the
completion of Creation as described in the Bible, and
the emancipation of the Jews from Egyptian bondage.

The Sabbath meals are turned into feasts. And the very
poorest make an effort beyond their means to honor the
Sabbath with good food and special dishes. Even the bread
served on the Sabbath is made richer, whiter, and shaped
differently than the daily bread.

In orthodox homes the Sabbath is welcomed as a queen
and bride. During the Sabbath it is customary to speak

RITUAL OBJECTS USED AT THE
END OF THE SABBATH
Spice box, braided candle, cup of wine

softly and never in anger, as if there were an honored guest in the house. And when the day is over, the departure of the Bride Sabbath is accompanied by a ceremony.

Just as the first star appears in the sky, the head of the family brings out a small box of fragrant spices. A glass is filled to the brim with wine. And a ceremonial candle, used especially for this occasion, is lit. The family is silent. They inhale the aroma of the spices. Each one comes close to the lighted candle to hold his fingers near enough to throw great shadows on the ceiling.

Then the head of the family chants solemnly:

"Blessed art Thou, O Lord our God, King of the Universe, Who made a distinction between light and darkness, between the holy and the ordinary, between the Sabbath and the weekday."

Then he dips the tip of the candle into the wine to extinguish the flame.

The Sabbath is over.

And everybody feels a little sad at that moment, as one would feel when parting from a good friend after a joyful visit.

Friday, Saturday and Sunday

The Jews observe the Sabbath on Saturday in the belief that on that day God rested after the six days of Creation; and that he gave this day of rest as a gift to the people of the earth with the Ten Commandments.

Christians observe the day of rest on Sunday in the belief that the Resurrection of Jesus took place on that day in the week. It is called the Lord's Day, or the Christian Sabbath.

The Moslems observe Friday as the weekly holiday in the belief that Adam was born on that day, and that on a Friday he went up to Paradise.

The rest of the people of the world do not have a Sabbath of their own.

Strangely enough, the Jews have no names for the days of the week, except the Sabbath. The other days are called merely "the first day," "the second day," and so on. But, unlike any other people, they have a name for each week in the year. The name of the week comes from the opening word in the section of the Scriptures read in the synagogue during the Sabbath service.

Ten Days of Repentance

At the end of the summer, close to the autumn equinox, the Jews celebrate a holiday that lasts for ten days, called the Ten Days of Repentance. It is also known as the Solemn Days, the High Holy Days, and the Fearful Days.

The first of the ten days is called Rosh Hashonoh, meaning "the beginning of the year" — which it really is not.

For it comes on the first day of the *seventh* month of the Jewish calendar.

In the distant past the Jews probably welcomed the new year as a great festival on the first day of their first month, Nisan, which arrives soon after the twenty-second of March. It was a spring festival observed by most of the early nomadic people. But after they settled on land in Palestine, the Jews began to observe New Year in the autumn, when the first rains came and the soil was plowed for the winter grain.

Like so many ancient nations, the Jews kept the old nature holidays but gave them new names and found new reasons for celebrating them. The first day of their seventh month, they now claimed, was the sixth day of Creation; it was the day Adam was made out of clay; it was also the birthday of Abraham and Isaac and of Jacob; it was the day Joseph was released from prison in Egypt; and it was the day Moses first appeared before Pharaoh, demanding that the king let his people go out of Egypt.

In the Bible this holiday is called "The Day of the Sounding of the Ram's Horn" — the call from the Heavenly Shepherd to listen to the Voice of God. The sounding of the horn is to rouse those who have fallen asleep in their duties or have neglected the truth revealed to them in the Commandments. It is a solemn blast of horns and a grave proclamation of a memorial day.

And this is the reason given for the solemnity of the New Year:

The Book of Life

There is a Book of Life in heaven, the Jews believe, in which every deed, word and thought of every human being, the year long, is recorded.

On the first day of the month of Tishri, the Book of Life is opened and the good and evil acts, words and thoughts of each person are examined. On the basis of this record the fate of each person for the coming year is inscribed.

That is why the Jewish New Year greeting cards always say, in Hebrew: "May you be inscribed for a good year!" And when Jews meet on this holiday season, they greet each other with the same wish.

But even though a man may have sinned, if he confesses his sins and repents during the days of repentance that begin with the New Year, his fate, already inscribed in the Book of Life, may be changed at the last moment, before the verdict is sealed.

Vicarious Sacrifices

The New Year is celebrated for one day by Reform Jews and for two days by the Orthodox. But all try to recall their sins of the past year. They pray. They make New Year's resolutions.

In the synagogue the ram's horn is blown, and God is asked to forgive the sins of the congregation for the sake of

Abraham, who was willing to sacrifice his beloved son Isaac to prove his faith.

At home the family gathers for a festive meal. After the blessing of the wine (with which every Sabbath and holiday feast begins), the head of the family cuts the holiday bread and passes it around. Each member of the family takes a small piece of bread and dips it into honey, and they say to each other, as if it were a toast: "For a sweet New Year!" But everybody is solemn and there is no merrymaking.

On the afternoon of the first day of the New Year, the men gather near a river or the shore of a lake to "cast all their sins into the depths of the sea." They empty their pockets and shake out the corners of their garments as they recite their eagerness to free themselves of wrongdoing.

After the New Year, the Days of Repentance continue. People go to work and the children go to school. Neighbors visit each other to make peace and to ask forgiveness if any have been wronged. And on the evening preceding the ninth day, some Orthodox Jews offer up vicarious sacrifices, a custom dating back to very early times.

The following morning is spent in visiting neighbors, friends and business acquaintances. People stop just long enough to shake hands, ask each other's forgiveness, and wish each other again a Happy New Year.

But this time they do not say: "May you be inscribed for a good year!" For they believe that on the last Day of

Repentance the verdict of every living being has been sealed. They say, therefore: "May your *fate be sealed* for a good year!"

The Day of Atonement

The tenth Day of Repentance, the most solemn day of the Jewish year, is called: Yom Kippur — the Day of Atonement.

Before sunset people gather for the feast which precedes the fast of this solemn day. And with the appearance of the first star in the sky, men, women and children gather in the synagogues.

In the Orthodox synagogues the halls are filled with huge candles which burn for twenty-four hours in memory of the dead. The women, separated from the men, are dressed in white. And the men cover themselves with their white prayer-shawls. For some time the entire congregation stands in silence. The Ark is opened and the Holy Scrolls are brought out. Then the cantor begins the mournful prayers that are to last all evening and throughout the next day — from the beginning to the end of the great fast.

Eight times during the Day of Atonement, the congregation makes a confession to every kind of sin and wrongdoing just in case they have committed any of the sins unknowingly. The confessions are made by the congregation as a whole, and forgiveness is asked for the congregation as a whole. And during the silent prayers of the Yom

BLOWING THE RAM'S HORN

Based on an eighteenth-century engraving

Kippur services, everyone prays that the entire human race, as nations united, may do God's will with a perfect heart.

When the first star appears in the sky, the ram's horn is blown in one long steady note.

The Day of Atonement is over.

People hurry home to break the fast that has lasted since sunset of the day before. And as they leave the synagogues they stop to wish each other:

"Le-Shonoh Tovoh Tikosemu!" (May your fate have been sealed for a good year!)

The solemn days are at an end.

In the Reform synagogues the services are quite different. Men and women are not separated. The atonement prayers are more formal. But the day is still a great fast and very solemn.

The Festival of Booths (Succoth)

Five days after the Day of Atonement, early or late in October, comes a Jewish holiday which is nine days long.

This holiday too is very, very old, for we are told about it twice in the Bible. It is called Succoth, which means "the holiday of booths," or "the holiday of tabernacles." But in the Bible it is called simply "the festival." And though it is called *the* festival, it is really several festivals in one.

"We Were Slaves in Egypt—"

There is one event in their history that the Jews never forget. Every Sabbath, at the blessing of the wine, they repeat their "remembrance of the departure from Egypt." And in several of their great holidays they commemorate events connected with their emancipation from slavery.

Succoth is one of these holidays.

For when the Jews came out of Egypt, according to the Bible, they wandered in the desert for forty years before they reached the Promised Land. During these years they lived in makeshift shelters made of dry palms and whatever branches they could find.

In the Bible they were enjoined to dwell in booths seven days each year in remembrance of the years of wandering and hardship.

After the Jews had settled in Canaan, they discovered that the autumn, when Succoth was celebrated, was also the time when they gathered in the crops. And they turned Succoth into a double celebration: they were grateful that they were no longer wanderers in the desert; and they offered thanks for the gathering in of the crops. It became the Jewish Thanksgiving.

The Succah

There is a beautiful custom connected with this holiday: Several days before it arrives, the families that observe it build a booth, or *succah*. Some *succahs* are built in gardens, where the people have gardens; or on roofs, where the roofs are flat; or the porch may be converted into a *succah* for the duration of the festival.

THE *ETHROG* AND THE *LULOV*

The entire family turns out to decorate the *succah* with strings of bright berries, garlands of long-lasting flowers, Indian corn, ripe pomegranates and clusters of grapes. The roof of the *succah* is covered with every variety of green branches.

Then a table is covered with a bright cloth and set for the holiday. In the center of the table appears the traditional bowl filled with the autumn fruits of the land. Near it is placed a pretty dish filled with cotton wool in which nestles a bright and fragrant citron; and near the dish lies a sheaf of long palm fronds, fastened with myrtle and willow twigs. The citron is called an *ethrog;* and the sheaf, a *lulov.*

In the *succah* the family gathers for all its meals during the festival. And every morning (except on Saturday), each member of the family, in turn, picks up the citron with the left hand and the sheaf of palm fronds with the right, and presses both hands close together. Then a special blessing is pronounced, while the hands are pointed toward the east and south, the north and west, and up and down; showing that the Jews believe that God is everywhere.

When the Skies Open at Midnight

The seventh day of this festival has a name of its own, Hoshana Rabah, the Day of Great Help. It is the day when the palm fronds and the willow and myrtle are given to the children. They make rings and bracelets, bows and tassels out of the palm fronds, to be worn as charms and amulets.

But more important to the children than the charms is the midnight of Hoshana Rabah. For exactly at midnight on the seventh day of Succoth the skies open. And anyone who makes a wish exactly at that moment when the skies open will have his or her wish come true.

The Eighth Day That Was Added

With Hoshana Raba the Holiday of Booths is really over. But two days have been added, two separate holidays that have nothing to do with Succoth or with each other.

The eighth day is called Shamini Atzereth, which simply means "the eighth day that was added." It is a festival dedicated to prayer for rain, for in Palestine the crops of spring depended on the rains of October.

Nothing very much happens on this day. People do not work. They seem to rest and prepare for the exciting holiday that comes the following day.

The Torah Festival

The ninth and last day of this autumn festival is one of the happiest of the Jewish year.

It is not a holiday in memory of a great hero.

It is not a holiday commemorating emancipation from slavery or the gaining of independence.

It is not a nature holiday.

It is a holiday dedicated to a book — really five books in one — called the Five Books of Moses. The Jews call the Five Books of Moses, the Torah. And the holiday is called Simchath Torah, "the rejoicing of the Torah."

Every Saturday a few chapters of the Five Books are read in the synagogue. It takes a full year of weekly readings to complete the Five Books. On this holiday the last of Deuteronomy is read. And the congregation starts again from the beginning by reading the first Chapter of Creation in Genesis.

This new beginning calls for a celebration.

One man in the congregation is chosen Bridegroom of the Torah; and another is chosen Bridegroom of Genesis. The Holy Scrolls on which the Five Books of Moses are written are taken out from the Ark and, led by the two bridegrooms, the entire congregation, singing and dancing, follows the Procession of the Scrolls. The adults are followed by the children, who carry flags bearing red apples stuck on top of each wooden staff. As the procession reaches the Ark, the Scrolls are handed to others to carry. This goes on until every member of the congregation has had the honor of bearing the Scrolls in the procession.

From the synagogue, the people leave in groups, going from one friend's home to another. Everywhere they are offered wine and pastries. And at each place they stop to sing and dance. The eating and the drinking, the singing and the dancing, goes on until late in the evening.

The Hindus have a unique holiday for their tools; and the Jews have a unique holiday for a book. But whereas the Hindus honor all tools, the Jews celebrate only one book — the Torah. Without air, they say, people cannot breathe; and without the Torah, people cannot live.

The Celebration of a Miracle (Hanukkah)

Toward the end of December, close to the winter solstice, there is an eight-day holiday which is celebrated by the Jews in remembrance of a miracle that took place in Palestine over 2100 years ago.

In those days there lived a tyrant whose name was Antiochus the Syrian, who hated all nations other than his own. And he vowed to destroy all faiths but his own. Many of the nations he conquered bowed to his will. But the Jews resisted him.

Antiochus tried to force them to give up their God and their sacred books. He desecrated their Temple in Jerusalem and ordered all the holy books burned, and with them all those who studied them.

During those terrible days there lived in Palestine, in the village of Modin, a man named Mattathias and his five good sons, each as mighty as a great oak. When the king's men came to Modin, demanding that the people offer sacrifices to idols, and threatening with death those who refused to obey, Mattathias slew the soldiers. Then he called out to the people in a mighty voice:

"*Mi Komocho Be-Elohim, Adonoi!*" (Who compares with you among the gods, O Lord!)

The first letters of this clarion call in Hebrew (MKBEA) are pronounced "Maccabee"; and all the followers of Mattathias and his sons became known as Maccabees.

The Maccabees fled to the mountains, and from their hiding places harried the king's men. For years they made the life of the tyrant Antiochus bitter with vexation. And when Mattathias died, his son Judas took over the leadership of the Maccabees.

After seven years of fighting, Judas won a number of victories over the armies of the king. And he returned with his followers to Jerusalem, determined to cleanse the Temple and dedicate it once again to the One God.

But when the cleansing was completed and the time came to kindle the eternal light in the Temple lamp, they found only one tiny cruse of sanctified oil, which could not possibly last more than a single night. And eight days were required to prepare fresh consecrated oil.

They poured a few drops of oil from the little cruse into one of the eight cups of the Temple lamp, called the Menorah, and lit it. The next day they found the wick still burning brightly. They poured a few drops into the second Menorah cup and lit that one. On the second day both wicks were found burning brightly.

Each day a light was added, until all eight of the Menorah cups were lit. And the oil miraculously lasted throughout the eight days.

Judas and all the people made a great celebration of the cleansing of the Temple, of their victories over the tyrant, and of the miracle of the cruse of oil.

This festival is called Hanukkah. And every year, since that first celebration, men gather in their homes to light the Hanukkah lamp. They praise the Lord for delivering the weak out of the hands of the strong, the few out of

LIGHTING THE HANUKKAH LAMP

the hands of the many, and those who believe in God out of the hands of the wicked.

They think not only of the fate of Antiochus and his hosts. They also think of other tyrants on earth who oppress the weak, impose their will on others, and threaten with extinction those who resist them.

Hanukkah is a very gay holiday. Gifts are exchanged.

Good food is eaten. And the children are given small square spinning tops which have on their sides the Hebrew letters NGHS. These letters stand for the words: "*Nes Godol Hoyoh Shom.*" (A great miracle happened there.)

Some people say that the miracle refers to the cruse of oil that lasted for eight days.

Others say that an even greater miracle happened there. For a few men of faith and courage triumphed over a mighty and wicked host.

The New Year of the Trees (Hamishah Osar Bish'vat)

Each spring the Jews celebrate the New Year of the Trees, just as the Chinese each spring celebrate the Birthday of the Flowers. This festivity is a children's holiday which comes on the fifteenth day of the Hebrew month of Sh'vat, and is called Hamishah Osar Bish'vat.

In ancient Palestine it was customary to plant a tree when a child was born: a cedar for a boy, and a cypress for a girl. When the children grew up and were married, branches from their own trees were cut and placed upon the bridal canopy, for good luck. Between birth and marriage they cared for their own trees. Through this custom every one learned to love trees. And trees were honored with a New Year's of their own.

In our own times the children of Israel plant trees on Hamishah Osar Bish'vat. And wherever Jewish children may be they sing songs to trees, to fruit trees in particular, and they feast on fruits native to Palestine — figs, dates, almonds, and the long brown pods which grow on the carob tree, and are known as Saint-John's-bread.

The Feast of Esther (Purim)

Very early in the spring, on the fifteenth day of the month of *Adar,* comes a holiday called Purim, which Jewish children await with the same excitement that Christian children await Christmas and Hindu children await Holi.

Purim is a time for gift-giving and for great fun. On no other holiday are so many sweets served — sweets which are made only on this holiday. And on no other holiday do the people, young and old, feel so lighthearted and ready for pranks, for music, and for laughter.

Bands of musicians roam the streets in some places, and go from home to home, to play for a while and to receive a reward. In practically every Jewish Community Center traditional comedies are presented that have a special meaning on this festive day. Carnivals and masquerades are in order. And wherever one goes there is fun and frolic.

Strangely enough, this feast began as a fast.

On this day, many centuries ago, Moses the Lawgiver ascended Mount Abarim in Moab, and from there was

PURIM MASQUERADER
Based on a print from Prague, 1741

taken to Paradise. The day Moses left this world would ordinarily be a very sad and solemn fast.

The story of how this fast of the fifteenth of Adar became a great feast is one the Jews never tire of telling. They have a book about it in their Bible, called the Book of Esther. And many other books have been written to explain the book in the Old Testament.

On Purim the Book of Esther is read and the many legends which were added to this book are related. Some parts are enacted in pageants, so that the story about Purim has become a great part of this holiday.

It is a story within a story, within a story. And this is how it is told:

The Queen Who Lost Her Crown

Once upon a time there was a very wicked king, named Ahasuerus, son of Darius the Median. Darius was king of Persia only. But his son, Ahasuerus, conquered province after province and country after country, until he was king over one hundred and twenty-seven nations, from Ethiopia to India.

In the third year of his reign the king ordered a feast in Shushan, his capitol, for all the princes and governors of the nations he ruled, and for the many thousands of ministers of his domain. For the king wanted to show off all the wealth he had obtained in battle.

So great were his riches, it took the guests one hundred and eighty days to see the royal display. Then the guests gathered in the palace gardens of spice trees decorated with rubies and diamonds and strings of pearls. There each guest was given a golden goblet filled with wine and each prince of a province proposed a toast to the king.

The king drank to each of the one hundred and twenty-seven toasts, and after seven days of toasting, Ahasuerus was in his cups. He began to boast. Anything anyone had, said the king, he had more of it. Anything anyone could do, said the king, he could do better. Anything that belonged to him, said the king, was finer and more beautiful, whether it was a crown, or a horse, or a peacock in the garden.

"What about the queen?" asked the princes.

"My Queen Vashti is the most beautiful woman in the world!" boasted the king. And he immediately sent five eunuchs to summon the queen.

The eunuchs soon returned with this message:

"I, Queen Vashti, am a descendant of King Belshazaar whom wine never made so foolish as to command his queen to appear before his guests wearing only a crown and carrying a goblet in her hand!"

The queen's message infuriated Ahasuerus. And he ordered Vashti driven from the palace and banished from his kingdom.

Contest for a Queen

Thus King Ahasuerus found himself without a queen and very lonely. He sent out three thousand, three hundred and thirty-three messengers, who spoke the seventy languages of the world, to seek out all the beautiful maidens in each kingdom and bring them to Shushan. The one that found most favor in the eyes of the king, it was announced, would be chosen queen to take Vashti's place.

Thousands of contestants arrived in Shushan from the four corners of the earth. On the appointed day, the king seated himself upon his throne, and the beautiful maidens passed before him. For hours and hours they passed. But the king could not make up his mind. They all looked equally beautiful.

Then came one girl before him who appeared different from all the others. And the king came down from his throne to speak to her.

"What is your name?" he asked.

"My name is Hadassah," she replied. "But my uncle calls me Esther."

The king placed the queen's crown upon Esther's head to signify his choice.

And that is how it came to be that Hadassah, called Esther, niece of Mordecai, the Jew who came to Shushan from Jerusalem, became the queen of the greatest kingdom on earth.

How Haman Became Chamberlain

In those days King Ahasuerus entrusted all his affairs to his chamberlain, Haman.

Haman was born in Tarshish. He was a very poor man and came to Tustar to enroll in the service of the king. But when he arrived, he found all the posts were gone, and Haman did not have the means with which to return home. He sat down at the entrance to the temple where the people brought their dead for the burial service.

Haman begged for alms of the mourners, and they gave them to him generously. Then he demanded a fixed amount of them, and people in their sorrow gave it to him. Until one day he blocked the way to the temple when a member of the royal family was brought for the burial service, demanding his fee. When the king heard of it, he ordered Haman brought before him for trial.

"Are you he who demanded tribute from a member of the royal family at the burial service?" demanded the angry king.

"I am he," said Haman, without regret and without shame.

"Who invested you with the authority to collect money from the mourners at the temple?" asked the king.

"And who ever forbade me to do so?" asked Haman. "If it is not forbidden, it must be allowed."

"How much have you collected so far?" asked the king.

"Enough to match the gold in your treasury," said Haman.

"If a man can gather so much for himself from the tax on the dead," thought the king, "how much more will he gather for his king from the tax on the living!"

And he appointed Haman as his chamberlain.

That is how it came to be that Haman the Agagite, the poor man from Tarshish, became the rich man of Shushan and chamberlain to the king.

Why Haman Hated Jews

The day Haman was appointed chamberlain, he issued a decree that all the people must treat him with the same respect shown to the king.

Everybody obeyed the decree. Only Mordecai, Queen Esther's uncle, refused to cross his hands upon his breast and bow before Haman when the chamberlain appeared.

"I am chief of princes and the king's chamberlain," said Haman in a rage. "Why do you refuse to bow before me?"

"I do not bow to one who vowed to be my slave," said Mordecai.

Haman looked closely at Mordecai. Then he grew pale. For he now remembered an incident that had occurred when he was a very young man and a soldier in the army. One day he and his companions were cut off by the enemy for many days. Haman's bag and gourd were empty of food and water. He went from soldier to soldier begging for food, and vowing to be a slave for life to him who would not let him die of hunger and thirst. Soldier after soldier refused. Then one, a Jew, offered to share his food and water with Haman.

Now Haman recognized in Mordecai that soldier.

The chamberlain went home in distress and told his wife Zeresh about his humiliation.

"You must kill Mordecai," said Zeresh. "And you must kill every Jew in the land."

"You are right," said Haman. "For as long as a Jew remains alive it might become known that I vowed to be a slave to Mordecai for a piece of bread and a sip of water."

And from that day Haman hated all Jews and plotted to destroy them.

How Esther Saved Her People

Each day Haman embittered the king's mind against the Jews.

"There is a certain people scattered in all the provinces of our nation," said Haman, "who are proud and haughty. They do not marry our daughters nor allow theirs to marry us. If a fly falls into the cup of one of them, he throws it out and drinks the wine; yet if my lord the king were to touch that cup, he would not touch the cup nor drink from it."

"Who are these people?" asked the king.

"The Jews," said Haman. "Let me send out a decree to kill them, destroy them, root them out."

"I am afraid of their God," said the king.

"Fear not, my king," said Haman. "Their God is angry with them or He would not have dispersed them among so many nations."

"On what day do you plan to destroy them?" asked the king.

"The Jews loved Moses more than any other man on earth, and the day he died is a day of great mourning for them. Moses died on the fifteenth day of their month of Adar. That would be a good day to destroy them."

Haman wrote out the decree; and Ahasuerus signed it.

When Mordecai heard of the wicked decree, he rent his clothes and sent word to Queen Esther. The queen dressed in sackcloth and sat down in ashes to pray. For three days she prayed. And on the fourth she arose, adorned herself in her royal garments, placed the crown upon her head and, accompanied by two handmaidens bearing her train, she went to see the king.

Her lovely face was serene and cheerful, but her heart was full of anguish and fear. For anyone who dared appear uninvited before the king was doomed to die, unless the king placed his scepter upon the intruder. And as Esther entered the throne room and looked up at the king in his robes of majesty, glittering with gold and precious jewels, she saw that his face was stern. The queen fainted.

The king leaped from his throne, placed the scepter on Esther's neck, and lifted her into his arms.

"What is the wish that brought you here?" asked the king, as she revived. "For whatever you want, even unto half of my kingdom, it shall be yours."

"Not part of your kingdom is my wish, but that you honor me tomorrow at a banquet," said Esther. Then she saw Haman standing nearby, and she added: "And the prince of princes, Haman, shall accompany you."

The following day, when the king's mood was mellow

with food, and his heart light with wine, the queen turned to him and said:

"My lord, yesterday you said you would grant my wish even unto half of your kingdom. Will you now grant me my life?"

"What words are these? Who dares attempt anything against your life?"

"He sits beside you," said Esther and pointed to Haman.

The king left the table in wrath and went into the garden to consider her accusation. When he returned he found Haman upon his knees, kissing Esther's hands, and she trying to pull away from him.

"Have you gone so far in your impudence as to raise your eyes to the queen?" asked the king in a rage.

He called the guards and ordered them to take Haman away and execute him. And at the same time, upon Esther's request, he revoked the decree Haman had issued against the Jews.

Then the Jews of all the one hundred and twenty-seven provinces of Ahasuerus' kingdom turned the fifteenth of Adar, a day of mourning, into a day of rejoicing. They named the holiday Purim, which means "the casting of lots," because Haman had cast lots to decide on which day to destroy the Jews. They also called it the Feast of Esther, and included her name among the seven prophetesses of Israel.

So beloved is Esther to the Jews that more has been

written about her in their sacred books than about any
other woman in their history.

And the Feast of Esther is their most beloved holiday.

The Great Celebration (Passover)

The arrival of the holiday called Passover is as welcome to the Jews as spring, which is exactly the time of
year when this holiday comes.

For days before Passover, preparations for the holiday
begin in every home. The house is thoroughly cleaned,
every candlestick and metal ornament is polished, and
all the dishes and silverware are scoured until they gleam.
And Orthodox Jews have a complete set of dishes, kitchen-
ware and silverware which are used only during the eight
days of this holiday.

The day before Passover the father and children go
through the house for a thorough inspection, to clear it
of all leavened bread or any crumbs of bread. For the
special bread eaten on this holiday consists of flat biscuits
made of wheat flour and water, called "matzoth." No
leavened bread is permitted to be brought into the house.

On the evening when the holiday begins, the fifteenth
day of the month of Nisan, every Jewish home is ready for
a very elaborate ritual. The ceremonial evening meal lasts
for hours and is part of a pageant in which each member

of the family and each guest takes part. This festive meal is called the Seder, meaning "the order." For everything in the Seder is as fixed as in a Chinese classic play and everything in the ceremony has symbolic meaning.

Near the head of the table, three matzoth are placed one on top of another and covered with an embroidered cloth, made especially for this purpose. The number three stands for unity in Jewish ceremonies. In the center of the table a large platter bears, arranged in a fixed order: a bone, an egg, some grated horseradish, a mound of grated apples mixed with nuts and honey, and a sprig of parsley. And near this platter is placed a small bowl of salted water.

At each plate stands a goblet, and by its size one can usually guess the age of the person who must drain it four times during the evening, for the younger the person, the smaller the goblet. And the very largest goblet of them all, filled with wine, stands in the middle of the table, and no one touches it during the entire evening. For this large goblet belongs to Elijah, the most beloved of all the prophets. During the ceremonies of the evening the door is opened and Elijah is invited to come in to join in the Seder. The children watch Elijah's goblet very carefully, and when they notice the wine quiver, they know that that is the moment when the prophet sips it.

Near each plate there is a small book, called the Haggadah, or the Passover Story. In the United States and in other English-speaking countries, this book is printed in Hebrew on the right side and English on the left.

The ceremony begins with the blessing of the wine; and after a short while the youngest member of the family asks the four traditional questions about Passover and the Seder:

"How does this night differ from all other nights?

"On all other nights we eat bread and matzoth; why on this night do we eat only unleavened matzoth?

"On all other nights we eat herbs of any kind; why on this night do we eat only bitter herbs? On other nights we do not dip our herbs in salt water; why on this night do we dip them twice?

"On all other nights we eat either sitting or reclining; why on this night do we all recline?"

And the father explains:

"We were slaves to Pharaoh in Egypt; and Moses was sent down to free our people from bondage.

"But although Moses performed many miracles before Pharaoh to prove that he came at God's command, Pharaoh would not believe him. Then God had Moses send plagues upon the land of Egypt until the king would relent. Nine terrible plagues were inflicted upon Egypt. Still Pharaoh would not let the Hebrews go.

"And a tenth and last plague was decreed by God. At midnight on the fourteenth day of the month of Nisan, all the firstborn in Egypt were to die. But the Hebrews who lived among the Egyptians were given a sign to place on their doors so that the Angel of Death would *pass over* their houses and spare their firstborn.

"On that fateful night, Pharaoh's own son was smitten, and at last the king told Moses to gather his people and leave Egypt at once.

"Moses and his people left Egypt so hurriedly that they had no time to prepare bread for the journey. They mixed flour with water and took the unleavened bread along on their journey out of bondage.

"And that is why the day when the Angel of Death was ordered to *pass over* the homes of the Hebrews became the festivity of their emancipation from slavery, and is remembered each year by the eating of unleavened bread."

Then the head of the family explains the meaning of the ceremonial platter on the table.

The bone is a symbol of the paschal lamb; the egg, a symbol of the sacrifice offered on this night in the Temple of Jerusalem, many centuries ago; the horseradish is to remind the Jews of the bitterness of slavery; the grated apple and nuts are made to resemble clay or bricks, which the Jews in Egypt had to make for Pharaoh's buildings; the salt water is for the tears they shed in slavery; and the sprig of parsley stands for the coming of spring, to remind them that there is hope in the world.

And during the Seder, when the ten plagues that afflicted Egypt are enumerated, each member dips the little finger of his right hand into his cup of wine, called the Cup of Joy, and spills a drop. This is a symbol of the belief that though the Egyptians deserved punishment, the Cup of Joy is diminished by the thought of the plagues. For one must never rejoice in the suffering of human beings, even if they are wicked.

After the questions are answered and the story is told, the rich and festive meal is served. The feast is eaten very slowly, to symbolize that the Jews are now a free people and no longer slaves who can be compelled to hurry.

After the meal traditional songs are sung by the entire family. They sing:

> Who knows one?
> I know one! One is our God both in heaven and on earth.
> Who knows two?
> I know two —

And they go on to thirteen, which is the number of the qualities of God.

Then comes the final song for which the children have been waiting all evening. It is about a little goat that Father bought for two coins. This song is similar to "The House That Jack Built." It goes on for a long time, and ends with:

> Then came God
> And smote the Angel of Death,
> Who slew the slaughterer,
> Who killed the ox,
> Who drank the water,
> That quenched the fire,
> That burned the stick,
> That beat the dog,
> That bit the cat,
> That ate the little goat,
> That father bought with two coins.

THE SEDER

*Based on a miniature from
the Darmstaedter Haggadah,
fourteenth century*

The Passover lasts for eight days. But the most exciting part is the pageant of the ceremonial Seder of the first evening.

Scholars' Day (Lag B'omer)

Early in the spring, on the eighteenth day of the month of Iyar, the Jews celebrate a holiday which is considered the luckiest day on which to get married. Those already married, or too young to marry, go out on this day to the woods or parks for picnics and outdoor games. Young boys and girls are usually accompanied by their teachers on these picnics. It is customary for them to bring bows and arrows and engage in contests of skill. At the end of their games, when they settle down, they listen to the retelling of the story of this celebration.

Long ago, nearly two thousand years ago, the Romans conquered Palestine and forbade Hebrew scholars to teach or study their holy books. The penalty for disobeying this decree was death.

One great scholar, Simeon Bar Yohai, refused to obey the edict and escaped with his son to a cave in Galilee. There they studied to their hearts' content for thirteen years, living on carob pods and other wild fruit, and the water of a spring that had appeared miraculously in their cave. Once each year Simeon's many followers came to visit their beloved teacher. And, fearing that the Roman soldiers might become suspicious, they dressed as hunters, and carried bows and arrows.

Simeon Bar Yohai, before he died, asked his followers to celebrate rather than mourn his death. That is why the day he died is celebrated as a joyful outing, and bows and arrows are brought to the Lag B'omer picnics.

In Israel, the pious make a pilgrimage to Meron, where Simeon is buried. They chant psalms at his grave, and in the evening they light a huge bonfire which they keep burning until midnight. While the men and boys dance around the fire, the women throw silk scarves into the flames as a symbol of their love for the scholar Simeon and for all great and brave scholars.

In the United States, Lag B'omer is the first day of Jewish Book Week. For what better way is there to honor a scholar than by reading books?

The Pentecost (Shabuoth)

What five is to the Chinese, seven is to the Jews. It is a number of great meaning:

There are seven days in the week.

The universe consists of seven great planetary systems.

There are seven heavens.

There are seven kinds of dwellers in Paradise.

Seven things were created two thousand years before the creation of the world.

The human head has seven openings: two ears, two eyes, two nostrils and one mouth.

The life of man is divided into seven stages: infancy, childhood, boyhood, young manhood, the prime of manhood, middle age and old age.

Seven times each night the cock crows to call the sluggards to waken, and thus gives them seven warnings that he who loves sleep must learn to love poverty.

And the Jews have many other beliefs about the number seven — enough to fill a book.

More important even than seven, is seven times seven — the jubilee number — the number of great rejoicing. For that is the number of days that elapsed from the time the Jews left their bondage in Egypt to the time Moses received the tablets of the law on Mount Sinai.

The Reception of the Law

The reception of the two tablets of the covenant, on which were inscribed the Ten Commandments, is celebrated in a holiday called Shabuoth, the Holiday of the Seven Weeks. It is also known as the Pentecost, which in Greek means "the fiftieth," because it takes place on the fiftieth day after the beginning of Passover.

This holiday in a sense completes the celebration of the Passover. For on Passover the Jews were freed from bondage in Egypt; and on Shabuoth the freed slaves were made into free men by the Ten Commandments.

The Jews believe that the Ten Commandments which they received at Mount Sinai are so remarkable that, were all the people on earth to abide by them, the world would be devoid of evil and full of goodness.

There would be no theft.

There would be no murder or wars.

There would be no adultery.

There would be no falsehood.

There would be no envy.

There would be no idolatry.

There would be no worship of Mammon or other false gods.

There would be no taking the name of God in vain.

There would be no slavery.

There would be no false witnesses in the courts of justice. . . .

It would, indeed, be a very good world to live in.

The Grain Harvest Festival

After the Jews had settled in Canaan and began to tend their fields and orchards, they noticed that the Holiday of Weeks came at the time when the first fruits of the land ripened, and they called Shabuoth also the Holiday of the First Fruits. And since Shabuoth was the time, too, when the wheat and the barley was ripe for harvesting, it became known also as the Grain Harvest Festival.

For many centuries it was customary to take boys to school for the first time on Shabuoth, and the Ten Commandments were read to the new students as their first lesson, just as the Hindu boys are taught the Sanskrit alphabet on Basanta.

In recent years Shabuoth has been adopted as the day of confirmation.

In Israel Shabuoth is a very gay holiday. The streets of the cities and towns are decorated with flowers and green boughs. Youths march in parades carrying banners and singing songs. And the people watching the parades join in the singing. Then they all gather in the squares to dance the ancient dances. And everywhere they eat food made with honey and milk — the twin symbols of the Torah.

It is a very happy holiday.

V   THE CHRISTIAN HOLIDAYS

A Merry Christmas!

Of all the Christian holidays, the most loved and important by far is the one that comes exactly one week before the new year: Christmas.

For weeks before it arrives one can tell of its coming wherever one goes. Like the first day of spring, Christmas can be felt in the air. In the stores, the streets, the churches and the schools everybody seems to be full of excitement and expectation.

On the city common or the public square there appears the huge evergreen with its many gay decorations. In the schools preparations are made for the pageant of the Nativity. In the homes gifts are brought in furtively and secretly stored away. On doors and windows appear green wreaths and poinsettia-red ribbons. And everywhere are seen the venders of evergreens, holly and mistletoe. Everyone seems a little breathless. Young and old grow busier as Christmas comes nearer. The days are counted. In some store windows signs appear:

"*20 more days to Christmas!*"
"*19 more days to Christmas!*"
"*18 more days to Christmas!*"

And with each passing day the excitement mounts.

"*The Holly and the Ivy*"

At street corners and at store entrances stand jolly figures in red Dutch costumes trimmed with white, the Santa Clauses with false white beards, who ring bells and collect coins given as alms for groups dedicated to the poor.

In some towns large streamers float across the main street, wishing everyone who lifts his eyes *A Merry Christmas!*

Then the night before Christmas arrives and the family gathers round to trim the Christmas tree. The house is full of the smell of pine needles, sweets and packing. The floor is littered with strings of multicolored lights, glittering silvery tinsel, golden globes and silver stars. And, when the tree is finally trimmed, the tinsel streamers hanging like icicles and the richly colored globes gleaming in the branches, each one in the family brings out from all the secret hiding places gaily wrapped gifts and places them neatly under the tree. And, though they are not supposed to, everyone tries to guess what gifts await them — even the grownups.

In cold countries people hope for snow. Everyone dreams of a crisp and white Christmas. Even in warm countries the Christmas tree is decorated with white cotton and soap flakes to resemble snow.

Early on Christmas Eve, boys and girls, young men and young women, gather in groups and go out to sing carols in their neighborhoods. Their young voices ring out through the dark night, commingling with other voices that come from far away like echoes in a deep valley:

> The holly and the ivy,
> When they are both full grown —

Or they sing:

> Three kings came riding from a land afar,
> And they were led by the morning star —

Different Christian countries have carols of their own for this night. The words are different. But the sentiments are the same.

In many great churches and in the little churches, people gather solemnly for a midnight mass or to hear Handel's *Messiah*.

No one is too young and no one is too old, no one is too

poor and no one is too rich, not to be stirred by the arrival of Christmas Eve.

The Old Winter Solstice

Christmas is a very old holiday.

It clearly started as a celebration of the passing of the winter solstice, and the start of the sun's return journey from the north to the south.

All the early nations of the earth joyfully celebrated the arrival of this season in the sun's journey. The ancient Romans observed this time with a festival dedicated to Saturn, the god of agriculture, and it was called Saturnalia. This festival was observed with great merriment and abandon. Gifts were exchanged. And great liberties were allowed between freemen and slaves — just as the Hindus allow the breaking of the barriers between castes on certain holidays.

When Emperor Constantine decreed Christianity as the new faith of the Roman Empire, early in the fourth century, the Christians gave the holiday an entirely new name and an entirely new meaning.

They called the holiday the Mass of Christ, or Christ Mass, which was shortened to Christmas. And they declared that Christmas was the birthday of Jesus of Nazareth. Though the exact day and year when Jesus was born are not known, tradition has set the date as December 25, 4 B.C., according to our present-day reckoning.

For a long time some Christians refused to celebrate Christmas Day because it reminded them of the Roman Saturnalia. In the early days in New England the Puritans prohibited the celebration of Christmas. And on the law-books of New England a fine was established for anyone found feasting on Christmas Day or abstaining from work. The law remained on the books into the eighteenth century.

But now all Christians have accepted Christmas as a holiday, and the symbol of this holiday for most is the enchanting Christmas tree.

There are many legends to explain the custom of the Christmas tree. One legend claims that Martin Luther, the German leader of the Reformation, walked home one Christmas Eve and was so deeply moved by the beauty of the sky and the bright stars in the

SAINT NICHOLAS
On a Belgian pastry mold

wintry sky, that it seemed to him as if he saw the firma-
ment at night for the first time. He wanted to tell his wife
about it. And as the best way to tell it, he took a small
fir tree, decorated it with gold and silver, and lighted tiny
red candles in the green branches, then set the tree upon
the table. And that is how, according to this legend, the
Christmas tree idea was born.

There are just as many legends about Saint Nicholas,
whom we know by his Dutch name and costume as Santa
Claus. Curiously enough the German Little Christ Child
(*Christkindlein*) has somehow become the name Kriss
Kringle.

But the most beautiful legends of all are those about the
miracles that took place on the outskirts of Bethlehem, so
many centuries ago, when Jesus was born.

"Silent Night—"

According to one legend, Joseph the Carpenter and
his two sons, Simon and James, accompanied Mary from
Nazareth to Bethlehem, where they had come to register
for the census.

On the outskirts of Bethlehem, Mary said to Joseph:
"We must stop here, for my time has come. Go to the city
and find a midwife to assist me."

Joseph led Mary into a nearby cave, close to the tomb of
the matriarch Rachel. There he left her with his two sons

to guard the entrance of the cave, and he hurried on to Bethlehem.

Suddenly Joseph looked up at the sky and he saw that everything was without movement. The birds on wing were suspended in mid-air. The workers in the fields at their evening meal were not eating. The cutter of the bread was fixed in the act of cutting; the pourer of the drink remained fixed in the act of pouring; and the hand of the one who had started to convey food to his mouth did not reach the mouth.

At the river's edge Joseph saw lambs with outstretched necks, their mouths touching the water, but they were not drinking.

Everything in the world stood silent and still.

Joseph lifted his eyes toward heaven and he saw a star in the evening sky, larger and brighter than any he had ever seen before. The star was unlike any other star, for it was in the shape of a woman with an infant in her arms, and a crown of bright light rested on the infant's head. Then the star began to move. Joseph's eyes followed it with astonishment as it passed across the heavens and came to rest over the place where he had left Mary in the cave. There the star stopped.

And in that instant the lambs drank, and the men ate, and the birds flew, and everything in the world that had stood still and silent began to stir again.

Christmas is observed a little differently in various parts

THE FAMOUS CHRIST CHILD OF PRAGUE

of the Christian world. But everywhere the favorite song on Christmas Eve is:

Silent night, holy night —

A Happy New Year!

Exactly one week after Christmas comes New Year's Day. In the minds of many people these two holidays seem to go together as if they had something in common. Actually, of course, there is no relationship between them. Christmas is a deeply religious holiday, whereas New Year's Day does nothing more than mark the beginning of the civil year.

The date we celebrate as New Year's, like the date of Christmas, is an inheritance from the Romans.

Most ancient nations celebrated the new year with the coming of spring. And the early Romans, too, welcomed the new year early in March, close to the spring equinox.

But Julius Caesar changed the Roman New Year's Day from March to January, in honor of Janus, the god of all beginnings, the god of agriculture, and the keeper of the gates of heaven and earth. The first month of the year was named after Janus. And Julius Caesar decreed that the first day of the first month be dedicated to the Festival of Janus, and mark the beginning of the new year.

Two-faced Janus

Janus was represented among the Roman gods as having two faces. He was called Janus Bifors, meaning "Janus with the two faces." One face always looked back to the old year, and the other always looked forward to the new. In his right hand Janus held a key, with which he

JANUS ON A ROMAN COIN

closed the old year and opened the new; in his left hand he held a scepter, symbol of his power.

A great temple with immense gates was built to Janus. And when Rome was at war, the gates of the temple of Janus stood open. But when peace was declared, the gates were closed with great rejoicing.

There was also great rejoicing before the gates of the temple of Janus on New Year's Day when the people gathered to do homage to the god of all beginnings. Gifts were exchanged among friends. Resolutions to be friendly and good to each other were made. And the entire day was given to festivities.

When the Romans under Constantine accepted Christianity as their new faith, they retained the Festival of Janus as their New Year's Day. But they turned the feast into a fast and a day of prayer. It was decreed that the day should be spent in solemn meditation, in repentance, and in the making of good resolutions. It was a day for every Christian to turn over a new leaf.

For centuries New Year's Day remained a fast and a solemn day.

But not all Christians observed it. As late as the seventeenth century the Puritans of New England refused to observe New Year's Day because, said they, it reminded them too much of the wicked heathen god Janus. Some even went so far as never to mention January among the months of the year. They just called it First Month and nothing more — so hateful was Janus to them.

Fast into Feast

About three or four hundred years ago New Year's Day began to change slowly from a fast into a feast. In different countries throughout the Christian world there arose beliefs, superstitions and customs about New Year's Day. In England it became the custom to ring church bells to welcome the new year. First the old year was rung out with muffled bells and sorrowfully; then the new year was rung in loudly and joyfully. In England, too, began the custom of opening the doors at midnight on New Year's Eve to permit the spirit of the old year to depart and to let the spirit of the new year come in out of the cold.

In many countries the custom arose of giving or exchanging gifts on New Year's Day. This custom persists in France and in other European countries. In England the king or queen had the right to make it known that he or she would welcome gifts on this day. Many subjects took it as a command.

Queen Elizabeth of England — that is, Queen Elizabeth the First — according to record often found her royal warehouse bulging with gifts of every kind after the first of January.

The Dutch who came to settle in New York introduced the custom of making calls on New Year's Day. Usually the unmarried men called on the unmarried women. It was a good day for young men with thoughts of marriage to meet many eligible girls.

Slowly the first day of the new year became a holiday of great rejoicing — and more particularly New Year's Eve.

Everywhere there are parties. People come and go from one gathering of friends to another to wish them a happy new year. There is singing and there is dancing. Just before midnight everyone's glass is filled. People stand up. They watch the creeping minute hand. Their eyes are on the hand of Time.

Then suddenly the moment arrives. They all shout greetings. They shake hands. They kiss each other. They wish each other once again a very happy new year. And they sing:

Should auld acquaintance be forgot . . .

The parties break up slowly, long after the new year is in. And the next day is spent in visiting friends, in thinking of the year that is past, in resolving to make the coming year better than the year that has just passed into eternity.

It is the day of good intentions and firm resolutions.

Saint Valentine's Day

You would never think that the holiday of sweethearts, St. Valentine's Day, had anything to do with wolves. But it does.

Long ago, long before the Christian era, there were wolves roaming through the European countryside, killing cattle and sheep, and even menacing the farmers and their families. The wolf was a constant enemy.

For each enemy of theirs the Romans had a god-protector. The god who protected the Roman farmers from wolves was called Luperus the Wolf Killer. Once each year, on February 14, the Romans celebrated the triumphs of Luperus in a festival called Lupercalia. On this day a goat and a dog were sacrificed to the Wolf Killer, and the rest of the day was given to a winter festival of great rejoicing.

As time went on, this holiday became even more important to the Romans. For the dreaded wolf had become an object of great respect. Romulus and Remus, later the founders of Rome, were saved by a she-wolf who suckled the abandoned infants in a cave near Palatine Hill. The she-wolf, it was believed, was Lupera, wife of Luperus.

It was also believed by the Roman farmers (and it is still believed in sections of rural England) that on February 14 the birds begin to mate. And somehow this holiday of Lupercalia became also the right time for young people to choose their partners for the year. It became a sweethearts' holiday.

Wolves into Saint Valentine's Clothing

When Rome became a Christian country, the early Church Fathers wisely refrained from abolishing many of the Roman holidays. Those festivals most favored by the people were kept as Christian holidays by changing their names and their meanings. The holiday on the fourteenth of February was retained, except that the name was changed from Lupercalia, held in honor of Luperus, to Saint Valentine's Day, held in honor of a Christian martyr who was beheaded by Emperor Claudius in the year A.D. 270.

The old holiday with its new name took root, particularly in England. There it became very popular with all young men and young women whose thoughts turned to love early after the winter solstice.

On this day in England they played a popular game, called "Choosing of Valentines." This consisted of writing down the names of all the young women on pieces of paper, rolling the papers so that they could not be read, and placing them all in a bowl. Then the young men would gather around and each, blindfolded, would draw a name from the bowl. The girl whose name he drew would be his valentine and sweetheart for the coming year.

Very young boys and girls would dress up, pretending they were grown-ups, and would parade around in their neighborhoods singing:

> Good morning to you, Valentine,
> Curl your locks as I do mine,
> Two before and three behind,
> Good morning to you, Valentine!

So popular did Saint Valentine's Day become in England that we find it mentioned by many of Britain's great authors. Sir Walter Scott wrote a novel called *St. Valentine's Day*. And Shakespeare makes Ophelia, in *Hamlet*, talk wistfully about Saint Valentine's Day. So serious were the people about the Saint Valentine's letters lovers sent to each other, that a number of books were published to teach the proper sentiments to be expressed in such letters.

Later on, people stopped writing letters and began to

send out ready-made cards, with the right sentiments expressed in verse, and decorated with red hearts and blue ribbons and lace. This custom still persists.

VALENTINE CARD, MIDDLE NINETEENTH
CENTURY

*Valentine collection, Children's Room, New York Public
Library*

In the United States Saint Valentine's Day cards have become extremely popular. Millions of them are sent each year.

As with any holiday that has been observed for centuries, many beliefs have grown up around Saint Valentine's Day. And here is one of them:

If a boy is in love with a girl,
Or a girl is in love with a boy,
And he should find her
Or she should find him
Asleep on Saint Valentine's Day,
Should he wake her, or she wake him, with a kiss —
That is certain to bring good luck!

Easter

The three most important events in the Christian faith are: the birth of Jesus, the Crucifixion and the Resurrection.

Christmas celebrates the first event.

Easter celebrates the other two.

Easter begins long before Easter. Forty days before Easter Day, many Christians (the Anglicans, the Roman Catholics and the Greek Orthodox) start a long and solemn fast, called Lent, which in some ways resembles the Jewish Ten Days of Repentance.

Lent begins with Ash Wednesday. The very devout literally fast throughout the forty days of Lent, except for Sundays, when it is forbidden to fast. Those who do not actually fast throughout this period do not touch meat, nor do they engage in any merriment or personal celebrations. It is a season of penitence and self-denial, similar to the Jewish Days of Repentance.

The most solemn week of the Lenten period is Passion Week, or Holy Week. This week begins with Palm Sunday, commemorating Jesus' arrival in Jerusalem for the celebration of Passover, when his followers reverently strewed his path with palm branches; and it reaches its most solemn moments on Good Friday, the day on which Jesus was crucified.

Though not all Protestants observe Lent, all Christians celebrate Easter Day, commemorating the Resurrection.

Easter Day invariably falls on a Sunday, the first Sunday after the full moon following the spring equinox, late in March.

The name of this holiday and the time it is celebrated have led people to believe that an earlier holiday existed on this day before the Christian observance. For many ancient nations joyously celebrated the end of winter and the "resurrection of the sun" at this season of the year; and some devoted this festival to Eostur, goddess of spring.

The Church Fathers turned this heathen holiday into the Christian celebration of the Resurrection. And Christians the world over observe this day with great rejoicing. Some greet each other with: "Christ is risen! Christ is risen!" And all think of Jesus, who conquered death so that those who follow him may gain everlasting life.

The Stranger on the Road

There are as many beautiful legends about the Resurrection as there are about the infancy of Jesus. And here is one of these stirring legends:

Two men walked along the dusty road from Jerusalem to Emmaus, seven miles away. The name of one was Zacchus and the name of the other was Cleophas. They walked in silence, for their hearts were heavy. And as they trudged wearily along, they were joined by a stranger going their way.

"You seem sad and discouraged," said the stranger to them. "Has some great grief befallen you?"

Cleophas turned his head and asked: "Are you a stranger in Judea? Have you not heard what has happened in this land?"

"What has happened?" asked the stranger.

"Have you not heard of the Prophet of Galilee, mighty both in word and deed, who came to drive the Romans from Jerusalem and become the King of the Jews?"

"Tell me about him," said the stranger.

"His name was Jesus," said Cleophas with a sigh. "He was born in Bethlehem. And his home was in Nazareth in Galilee. He loved the people more than himself. And he had the power to heal the sick and to comfort the sorrowing. The priests envied him his power and denounced him before Pilate. And last Friday Jesus was taken to Golgotha and was crucified in the Roman manner."

Cleophas fell silent, and Zacchus continued: "He died and was buried in a rich man's tomb, out in the garden of Siloam. That was three days ago. But this morning, when his friends went to the tomb, they found it empty. And now the news has gone out abroad that Jesus has risen from the dead. But it is also said that his friends have taken him away to make it appear that Jesus has risen."

They had reached Emmaus and the house where Zacchus and Cleophas lived. The day had waned and night was upon them. Cleophas and Zacchus invited the stranger to break bread with them and stay the night.

They sat down at the table. As the meal was served, the stranger broke the bread and blessed it in the name of Jesus the Christ. Zacchus looked at Cleophas and Cleophas looked at Zacchus in astonishment. Then they turned to their guest. But the stranger had disappeared.

The two men left their food untouched and hurried back to Jerusalem to relate that they had seen Jesus, who had risen from the dead; and that he had sat down with them to the evening meal and had broken the bread of life for them.

The Easter Parade

On Easter people go to church services and delight in the sight of great masses of Easter lilies that decorate the altars. For the Chinese the peony is the king of flowers and symbol of spring. But to the people in their churches on

Easter Day, the fragrant lily with its blossoms shaped like Gabriel's trumpet is the symbol of purity and the welcome harbinger of spring.

The churchgoers enjoy the flowers and the music and the sermon of the day. And from time to time they look about them to observe the gay clothes that people wear, since it has long been the custom for people to put on their newest clothes on Easter Day. And in many American cities the people coming out of the churches provide an involuntary fashion parade.

In countries where the Greek Orthodox Church dominates, a quite different parade is put on during Easter. The worshipers gather early on Saturday night in an elaborate ritual. And at midnight, led by their priests in richly embroidered vestments, carrying images and lighted candles in their hands, they go out into the night in search of Jesus. And after several hours of ceremonious search they return and the priest, with cross lifted high for all to see, sings:

"The Lord Jesus is risen!"

And all those present respond in a great outcry:

"He is risen, Christ our Lord!"

The bells overhead begin to ring, quick and loud, and the people embrace and kiss each other.

It is almost dawn when the people return home to eat the Easter bread with white cheese and honey and the richly colored hard-boiled eggs. Then they spend the day visiting neighbors and friends, where they leave a hardboiled egg of diverse colors and receive a colored egg in return. Families give as gifts to the next guests the eggs received from those who have just left.

But in the end, the children have many colored eggs with which to play.

Egg-rolling on the White House Lawn

The first thing that comes to mind as soon as one says Easter, is: eggs.

From the earliest days in man's history the egg has been accepted as a symbol of the universe. When a child is born in China, hard-boiled eggs are put into its first bath — one white egg if it is a boy; two eggs colored red, if it is a girl. These are to assure the child a long life, good health and abundant good luck.

The egg of Easter has become a symbol of the Resurrection. Colored eggs are used wherever Easter is celebrated. In some countries games have been devised in which these eggs are used especially on Easter Day or Easter Monday.

In the United States it has become a custom for the President and the First Lady to receive children on the south lawn of the White House for their egg-rolling game. If the weather is fair, thousands of children arrive in their best clothes, carefully carrying ornamented baskets full of colored eggs. The Marine Band plays for them. The President and the First Lady sometimes address the children and shake hands with some of them. The children wander

EASTER EGGS

From the Transylvanian Alps and the Carpathians

about the beautifully landscaped grounds. Some of the children bring with them bright balloons which are gleefully released in the air. But the egg game is most absorbing to them. They roll their eggs down the slopes, trying to hit the eggs rolled by others, for the owner of the unbroken egg is the winner. When their egg game is over, they play other games, aware that they have the freedom of the White House grounds only on Easter Monday.

May Day

The early Romans had a goddess of flowers and of spring whose name was Flora. Every year, early in May, the children of Rome filled Flora's temple. They came dressed in their brightest clothes, wearing garlands of flowers on their heads and carrying the flowers of spring in their arms.

In Flora's temple there was a huge marble column around which the children twined their garlands, and they placed their flowers on the altar of the goddess. Then they curtsied and danced around the column, singing hymns in praise of Flora.

Many years later the same holiday was elaborately celebrated in England on the first of May. But instead of a marble column in the temple of Flora there were set up in the public squares immense Maypoles, gaily decorated

DANCING AROUND THE MAYPOLE
After a French eighteenth-century tapestry

with bright streamers. On these Maypoles the children wove their garlands, and they danced around the poles and sang songs.

The early settlers of the United States brought over with them all their customs, their beliefs and their celebrations. And some of the English settlers did not forget May Day and the dancing around the Maypole. The Puritans, who disliked all the remnants of the Roman holidays to heathen gods, looked down upon the May Day celebration and urged their children on that day:

> Now take the Bible in your hand and read a chapter through,
> And when the day of judgment comes, the Lord will think of you.

But the holiday survived the Puritans' displeasure and is celebrated everywhere by children as a happy spring festival.

All Saints' Day

Many solemn holidays and fasts begin with a feast. Before the Day of Atonement the Jews gather at a family feast. And, preceding Ash Wednesday, which starts the forty-day Lent, comes Shrove Tuesday, when the tables groan with food and the homes ring with merriment.

And on the eve of the solemn All Saints' Day, people indulge in an evening of fun, unlike any other evening in the year. This is called Allhallow Eve, shortened to Halloween.

Halloween

Long, long ago the Celts, the first Aryan people who came from Asia to settle in Europe, celebrated the new year on the first of November. And, according to their belief, on the last night of the old year, the night of October 31, the souls of the dead were allowed to return to their homes. Also all the witches and the sirens, the demons, the hobgoblins, the trolls and every kind of evil spirit was allowed to roam the earth on this night.

It was a fearful night. And, until not so long ago, great bonfires were kept burning on this night in many parts of England. Men, armed with pitchforks and shouting loudly, frolicked around the fires to frighten the witches and evil spirits away. In some ways, their merriment around the bonfires was very much like the carryings-on of the Hindus on the night of Holi.

After many years, as people grew less superstitious, this evening was turned into a festival of parties for young people, who dressed in weird costumes, and on this night played games which were supposed to foretell whether they would marry or remain bachelors and spinsters for the rest of their lives. Many beliefs arose about how to conjure up the image of one's future wife or husband. Girls believed that if one sat at midnight before a mirror eating an apple, the image of her future husband would suddenly appear before her. If no image appeared it was taken to mean that the girl would remain a spinster.

In England, apples are in some way associated with this

CARVED PUMPKINS

night; and in the United States pumpkins are popularly used in rural areas for jack-o'-lanterns. The pumpkins are carved out to resemble faces; candles are placed in the hollowed-out pumpkins and lighted; and the children that carry them around on this night dress up in amusing or weird costumes, their faces covered with masks or painted to appear frightening. Groups of boys and girls used to roam the streets bent on mischief, marking cars with soap, and placing movable objects in unusual places. Now more often they knock on the doors of neighbors and ask for candy, with the warning, "A trick or a treat!" And the friendly neighbors, duly fearful on this Witches' Night, have the treats all ready.

In some rural areas, the community organizes a barn dance. The barn is decorated with carved pumpkins and

APPLE FISHING

cornstalks. Games are set up. Everyone appears in costume. Floating apples are fished out of a tub, by fishermen whose hands are tied behind them. The local talent supplies the music. And the dancing goes on till past midnight.

At midnight, All Saints' Day begins.

Lest We Forget!

In all religions there is a day set aside for remembrance of the dead.

All Saints' Day and All Souls' Day, which follows it, are the two days which are dedicated by Christians, and more particularly by members of the Roman Catholic Church, to the remembrance of the dead and as a day of sorrow and reverence for all the early Christians who died as martyrs for their faith.

Different ways of observing this holiday have been adopted in different Western countries. In some, one or both days are legal holidays. But in most places they are observed only as church holidays.

For many years in the past, it was the custom in some countries for each family to set the table with food, then leave for church, with the doors to the house left open. In church a special service was held for all the dead, and each worshiper prayed silently for the dead members of his own family. On returning home from church people expected to find the food gone. If the food remained untouched it was considered a very bad omen.

Thieves and beggars, of course, knew of the custom and swarmed into the unlocked houses as soon as the people left for church. They ate or collected the food. And some also helped themselves to the silverware and other household goods. This happened so often that the custom was finally abandoned.

Nowadays, in most countries, people bring flowers instead of food to honor departed kin. Just as we do on Memorial Day, which is devoted not only to the departed members of our families but to all the soldiers who died in all the wars to preserve the nation.

Thanksgiving Day

We often think of Thanksgiving as an American holiday, begun by the Pilgrims in Plymouth in 1621. At that time, so the story runs, the survivors of the *Mayflower* passengers celebrated their first harvest in the New World with a feast to which Governor Bradford invited the Indian Chief Massasoit and ninety of his braves.

That was the first Thanksgiving Day in the New World.

But actually a thanksgiving for the annual harvest is one of the oldest holidays known to mankind, though celebrated on different dates. In Chaldea, in ancient Egypt and in Greece, the harvest festival was celebrated with great rejoicing. The Hindus and the Chinese observe the gathered harvest with a holiday. And the Jews celebrate the ingathering of the crops as enjoined upon them in the Bible.

The Romans celebrated their Thanksgiving early in October. The holiday was dedicated to the goddess of the harvest, Ceres, and the holiday was called Cerelia. (That is where the word "cereal" comes from!)

The Christians took over the Roman holiday and it became well established in England, where some of the Roman customs and rituals for this day were observed long after the Roman Empire had disappeared.

In England the "harvest home" has been observed continuously for centuries. The custom was to select a harvest queen for this holiday. She was decorated with the grain of their fields and the fruit of their trees. On Thanksgiving Day she was paraded through the streets in a carriage drawn by white horses. This was a remnant of the Roman ceremonies in honor of Ceres. But the English no longer thought of Ceres or cared much about her. They went to church on this day and sang what all the people of the earth sing on their harvest holiday in different forms:

We plough the fields and scatter the good seed through the land,
But it is fed and watered by God's almighty hand. . . .

All good gifts around us are sent from heaven above,
Then thank the Lord, O thank the Lord for all His love!

The Pilgrims brought the "harvest in" to Massachusetts. But they gave it a slightly new meaning, since they were thankful for much more than their harvest. On that first year in Plymouth they were even more grateful for the friendship of the Indians, who might have destroyed them.

The Pilgrims also introduced the custom of eating turkey on Thanksgiving Day. For they found wild turkeys in great numbers and good to eat in the early autumn. We have adopted the custom, though we no longer find the turkey wild and free.

THE FIRST THANKSGIVING DINNER

In the United States, strangely enough, Thanksgiving Day is not established as a legal holiday. The President of the United States has to proclaim it each year; and he can shift it from the customary fourth Thursday in November to the third, or to any other Thursday of the month.

But so well loved is this holiday that it would be hard to abolish it. Thanksgiving Day is observed in every state in the Union, and in every village, town and city. The greatest feasts of this day are to be found on the farms and in rural areas.

Thanksgiving is a holiday of pleasant aromas. Every home is pungent with the commingling odors of apples and apple cider, pumpkins and pumpkin pie, brown sugar in the baking, autumn leaves and mountain herbs, and the slightly gamey odor of turkey roasting. It is a day for people with good appetites.

In many rural areas the holiday begins with a solemn church service, followed by a great feast at home, and ending with dances and games in some community center or a barn. If the revelry is held in a barn, the place is decorated with autumn leaves, fox grapes, apples and pumpkins. The country folk come in their worka-day clothes, though in some places they dress up like Pilgrims.

When all are gathered, a harvest queen is chosen and upon her head is placed a crown of autumn flowers or of winter berries. Then the dancing goes on around her. The fiddlers fiddle; the callers chant the steps; and the dancers dance the old folk dances.

They pause to eat. And they pause to sing old favorite songs. They sing:

There was an old man that lived in a wood,
As you can plainly see —
Who said he could do more work in a day
Than his wife could do in three —

Or they sing an old ballad like:

I'm just a poor wayfaring stranger,
A trav'ling through this world of woe —

Then they return to their dancing, and the merriment goes on.

The merriment of the harvest festivals is older than recorded human history. And the merriment of the harvest holiday is likely to continue, the world over, as long as men obtain their food from the good earth.

Roman Catholic and Greek Orthodox Holidays

The Christian religion is divided into three main branches: the Greek Orthodox; the Roman Catholic; and the Protestant.

In addition to the holidays celebrated by all Christians, the Roman Catholic and Greek Orthodox churches observe a number of fasts and feasts not recognized by most of the Protestant churches. Not all of these additional holy days are kept by both the Roman Catholic and the Greek Orthodox churches; nor are they observed on the same dates, because the Greek Orthodox Church still retains the old Julian calendar, which first differed by ten days and since 1900 differs by thirteen from the Gregorian calendar, generally observed in the Western world.

Here are the most important additional holidays:

ADVENT — This is the season of preparation for the Feast of the Nativity; it includes the four Sundays before Christmas.

THE OCTAVE OF CHRISTMAS — The eight days immediately following Christmas, from December 26 to January 2, dedicated to the Feast of Saint Stephen, the Feast of Saint John the Evangelist and the Feast of the Holy Innocents. But most important of all is the eighth day, dedicated to the Feast of the Circumcision of Jesus.

EPIPHANY — A three-in-one celebration in remembrance of the Adoration of the Magi, Christ's baptism in the Jordan, and the Miracle of Cana, when Jesus turned water into wine. Epiphany (January 6) closes the Christmas cycle of holidays.

CANDLEMAS — The Presentation of Jesus in the Temple of Jerusalem is remembered in a feast on February 2.

PENTECOST — Also called Whitsunday, and celebrated on the seventh Sunday after Easter to commemorate the descent of the Holy Ghost upon the Apostles on the Jewish Pentecost.

FEASTS OF THE BLESSED VIRGIN MARY — There are eight different feasts in honor of Jesus' mother. They come on

December 8, February 2, March 25, July 2, August 15, September 8 and 15, and October 7.

OTHER FEASTS — Throughout the year there are a number of additional feasts dedicated to Jesus, the apostles, the saints and the Church.

VI THE
MOSLEM
HOLIDAYS

Muharram

The youngest of the great religions of the world, the religion of the Moslems, is called Islam.

Mohammed is its Prophet; the Koran is its sacred book; Mecca is its most holy city; and its holidays are in many ways unlike the holidays of any other religion.

The Moslems (they *never* call themselves Mohammedans in their religious activities) follow strictly the counting of time by the moon, each month having 29½ days, and each year consisting of 354 days. They can never change that because the Prophet himself had a revelation in which he was told that good Moslems must follow only the lunar year — which means that their birthdays and holidays keep shifting eleven days each year. So every holiday may come in any season of the year, each year eleven days earlier. In thirty-three years they are back again where they started. The name of the first month of the Moslem year is Muharram.

And Muharram is also the name of a ten-day holiday that begins with the first day of the first month, which is the Moslem New Year Festival.

But not all Moslems celebrate the First of Muharram the same way. Moslems, like Christians, can be of any nationality. A man can be an American and a Christian; an Englishman and a Christian; an Italian and a Christian; a Russian and a Christian; or a Chinese and a Christian. Likewise a person may be a Jew by religion and an Israeli or an Englishman or a Frenchman or a member of any other nationality.

The same is true of Islam. There are Moslems in Pakistan, in Egypt, in Iran and all over Asia and parts of Africa. They have different nationalities, talk different languages, belong to different sects or denominations, but they are all members of the same religion.

When it comes to the celebration of their holidays, each nation, and each sect within each nation, has its own innovations and local customs. Just as Easter and Christmas are observed by all Christians, but observed differently by Protestants, Catholics and the Greek Orthodox of different countries; so also is the Moslem New Year observed quite differently by the Moslem sects of different countries. In some places the First of Muharram is purely a festival; and in others it is a very solemn fast.

The Tree at the Boundary

The Jews believe that there is a Book of Life in heaven in which all the deeds of all men are recorded. And each year, on the New Year's Day, this Book of Life is balanced; and on the basis of the past year's record, the future of every person for the coming year is inscribed.

But the Moslems believe that there is a wonderful tree, a lotus tree, which stands at the very boundary of Paradise. This tree has as many leaves as there are human beings in the world, each leaf bearing the name of a man or a woman or a child.

Early in the evening which begins the first day of Muharram, an angel comes and shakes this tree in Paradise. Many leaves fall down. And he whose name is inscribed on a fallen leaf will surely die during the coming year.

The Moslem New Year therefore begins with a prayer for mercy, and a prayer for the dead. They comfort each other with the Prophet's words: "Every soul shall taste of death, and you shall have your rewards on the day of Resurrection." And then they read from the sacred book what the Prophet Mohammed said about the certainty of the life hereafter.

Long before the tree at the boundary is shaken, long before New Year's Day arrives, the people prepare for its coming. Wherever possible, black tents are pitched. The tents are decorated, inside and out, with draperies, lamps, flowers and swords. Shops are closed early before the eve of the holiday. People neither bathe nor shave on this day, and they put on their clothes of mourning. Before the evening prayers they pour out into the streets to wish each other a good new year and to express the hope that their leaf will not fall from the Tree of Life in Paradise.

As they exchange good wishes, they exchange coins. If a coin is received before the good wish is uttered, that is considered a good omen, and the coin is kept for the rest of the year as a charm for good luck.

As night falls, everyone hurries to the mosque for the evening prayers and the reading from the Koran on death and resurrection.

O, Husain! O, Husain!

The Moslem Era does not begin with Mohammed's birth or his death; it begins with the day Mohammed, at the age of fifty-two, fled from Mecca to Yathrib, which has since been named Medina, meaning "the city of the Prophet." That happened on July 16, 622 A.D. The Moslems therefore count their time from A.H. or Anno Hegira: the year of the Flight.

And on the tenth of Muharram, 61 A.H. (October 9, 680 A.D.), about fifty years after Mohammed died, an event took place at Kerbela, some sixty miles from Bagdad, that certain Moslems remember with greater excitement than any in the life of their Prophet. For on that day Hazrat Imam Husain, son of Ali and Fatima, grandson of Mohammed, and third of the successors of the Prophet, rode into battle on his famous horse Duldul to fight against the forces of his enemy Yozid. And in that battle Husain's head was severed from his body by the sword of an enemy soldier.

His followers immediately declared that Husain deliberately chose his death so that through his martyrdom the True Believers in the teachings of Mohammed may enter Paradise.

Where Husain fell, there he was buried. The ground became sacred to the Moslems, and the city of Kerbela became a sacred city. The wish of certain Moslems since that day has been to be buried in Kerbela near the martyr Husain. Many Moslems come to die there; or their bodies are brought there for burial. And the city of Kerbela has become the world's largest burial ground.

On the First of Muharram, the story of Husain's martyrdom is recited in many Moslem halls. And the people listen to it with bowed heads, interrupting the recitation from time to time with outcries of:

"O, Husain! O, Husain!"

Outside the mosques and in the public squares half-naked men appear, their bodies painted red and black, who inflict many kinds of torture upon themselves. They pull out their own hair and they cut themselves with swords to suffer pain in remembrance of the martyrdom of Husain. This lasts for nine days. And on the tenth day of Muharram the murder of Husain is re-enacted in a religious drama that consists of some fifty scenes in the life of Husain and ends with his death on the battlefield. The spectators often become so excited that they threaten the actor who portrays 'Umar, the soldier who dealt Husain the fatal blow.

In some places a young boy on a white horse is paraded through the streets. The boy carries the standard of Hazrat Imam Husain's army. Both horse and rider are painted with streaks of red or smeared with blood. The parade moves with solemnity and people follow as if in a funeral procession, until the mosque or hall is reached where the pageant is being performed.

During all the days of Muharram the people distribute a variety of sherbet in memory of Husain's thirst on the field of battle at Kerbela.

(The commemoration of Husain's death is observed only by a branch of Islam whose followers are known as the Shiites; just as certain Christian holidays are observed only by Catholics.)

The tenth day of Muharram has a name of its own. It is called Ashura. And in addition to commemorating the death of Husain, it commemorates still another event, forever remembered by certain Moslems. This is not a sad event. On the contrary, it is a very happy one.

Ashura

The Koran devotes much space to a number of Biblical characters and events; and the Moslems celebrate a number of holidays in their honor. On Ashura, the tenth day of the first month, the Moslems remember with joy the safe landing of Noah's ark. For had not Noah landed safely, mankind would have disappeared from the face of the earth.

According to legend, Noah was so happy to come out of the ark and plant his feet on solid ground that he asked his wife to make a pudding with which they could celebrate the happy day. His wife gathered dates and raisins and figs and nuts and currants in great quantities. And she prepared not only the best but also the largest pudding ever made. And she named that pudding "Ashura."

And Moslem wives try their hardest on this day to prepare a pudding for their family as good and as huge as the pudding made by Noah's wife.

The Prophet's Birthday (Maulid an-Nabi)

There are several memorable birthdays on the Moslem calendar. The birth dates of some of Mohammed's spiritual successors, called caliphs, are celebrated. The birth of the

Prophet's adopted son, Ali, and of his only daughter, Fatima, are remembered in a festivity and with the distribution of alms. But the most joyous holiday of the Moslem year is the Birthday of the Prophet.

Since no one really knows when Mohammed was born, the date of his death has been adopted also as the day of his birth. Though this holiday, which falls on the eleventh day of the third Moslem month, Rabi'u l-aw'wal, is observed differently in the various Moslem countries, in all of them the birth of their Prophet is celebrated for nine days with great rejoicing. And in many cities this is the season for the most colorful fairs, parades and community feasting.

During the celebration of the Prophet's Birthday it is customary to relate the circumstances of his birth in Mecca and children are told of the miracles that took place on that holy night.

There are many legends about the miracles that attended the birth and childhood of many of the great leaders and prophets of old. There are the traditional stories about the Nativity of Jesus and the miracles during his infancy and childhood. There is that vast collection of birth legends called Jatakas, about Prince Sidhatta Gautama, who became the Buddha. And there are wonderful stories about Moses, Zoroaster, and other religious leaders, prophets, and apostles.

But about none of them are there so many legends and tales of miraculous events as about the birth and infancy of Mohammed. The Moslems are famous for their inventive imagination, and nowhere have they demonstrated it more than in the stories about their beloved Prophet Mohammed.

At the very moment Mohammed was born, so runs one legend, the mountains of the world began to dance and they sang: "There is no god but Allah!"

And the trees responded happily: "And Mohammed is his Prophet!"

Then every living thing — the fish in the water, the creatures on earth, and the birds on wing — called out together: "How bright is the star over Mecca! Now the world has a light to lead it!"

In those days the King of All the Seas was a creature named Tamoosa. This monstrous creature was so enormous that he had seven hundred thousand tails, and his back was so wide and so long that seven hundred thousand bullocks with golden horns romped about upon it, yet Tamoosa did not even feel them. And when Mohammed was born, Tamoosa began to splash the sea with all his seven hundred thousand tails and with such force that he nearly overturned the world in his great joy. And all the time he shouted *"La ilaha illa Allah! Mohammed rasul Allah!"* (There is no god but Allah! And Mohammed is the Prophet of Allah!) until Allah himself had to quiet Tamoosa down to save the world from destruction.

As soon as Mohammed was born, seven thousand angels brought a golden vessel filled with heavenly dew to his home. His mother bathed the newly born infant in the heavenly dew and forever after Mohammed was always clean.

And when Mohammed was a few days old, people came from all over the East and asked to see him. But when the infant's face was uncovered, the visitors quickly lifted their arms and closed their eyes to avoid being blinded by the dazzling light of the child's face, which was brighter than the sun.

These, and thousands of legends like these, are retold about Mohammed, particularly to the young, on the Festival of the Prophet's Birthday.

Ramadan

The religion of the Moslems rests on Five Pillars of Faith:

The duty to recite the creed: *There is no god but Allah, and Mohammed is his Prophet!* That is the First Pillar.

The duty to worship the One God in prayer five times each day. That is the Second Pillar.

The duty to distribute alms and to help the needy. That is the Third Pillar.

The Fourth Pillar is the duty of every True Believer to keep the Fast of Ramadan.

The Fifth Pillar is the duty to make the pilgrimage to Mecca at least once in a lifetime, if possible.

The keeping of the Fast of Ramadan is one fifth of the practice of the Moslem religion, called Islam.

Ramadan is the name of the ninth month of the Moslem year. The Fast of Ramadan lasts, not just one or two or even three days; but it lasts the entire month, from the first to the last of the month of Ramadan. Each day is given to fasting; and each night the fast is broken with a feast.

When does the fast begin each day? Who must fast? What destroys the good the fast does? And what is the reason given for this extraordinary fast?

No one has to guess the answers to these questions. They are given very clearly in the Koran, the Moslem sacred book.

One may eat and drink at any time during the night, "until you can plainly distinguish a white thread from a black thread by the daybreak: then keep the fast until night," says the Koran. If for any reason certain people can neither keep nor make up for the fast, their souls are not lost, but they "must redeem their neglect by maintaining a poor man" — presumably for a number of days equal to those on which they failed to fast.

Fasting is a test of faith in all religions. One fasts either to express great grief or to set the mind solemnly on spiritual matters without distraction from material pleasures. But simply abstaining from food and drink, said Mohammed, does not fulfill the duty of the Fast of Ramadan. The good acquired through the fast can be destroyed by five things: the telling of a lie; slander; denouncing someone behind his back; a false oath; and greed or covetousness.

These are offensive at all times, but most offensive during the Fast of Ramadan. For this is the month, says the Koran, "in which the Koran was sent down from heaven, a guidance unto men, a declaration of direction, and a means of Salvation."

The receiving of the Koran is to the Moslems what the receiving of the Ten Commandments from Mount Sinai is to the Jews.

One day, so the story is told, as Mohammed sat alone in the wilderness reflecting, the Angel Gabriel came to him with a golden tablet in his hands and commanded the Prophet to read what was inscribed upon it. And Mohammed read. What he read was the essence of the Koran. Just as the tablets of the Law received by Moses are the essence of the Old Testament.

During the Fast of Ramadan it is customary to spend much time in the mosques in prayer and in reading the Koran. And the Moslems recite with great feeling the last message the Prophet sent to his followers before he died:

Know that every True Believer is the brother of every other True Believer. All men are equal, for they are all of one brotherhood. Remember that Faith is in the heart! He who keeps the fasts but does not abandon lying and slandering, God does not care about his leaving off eating and drinking!

Ramadan is taken very seriously by all Moslems. But it is observed differently from Moslem country to Moslem country. In some places they fast during the day and pray and do penance; but during the night some permit themselves unbridled revelry.

THE END OF RAMADAN

In India, Moslem children paint their pet sheep

Even where the fast is observed solemnly throughout the month of Ramadan, the end of the fast is celebrated for three days with great rejoicing in a holiday called Id-al-Fitr. People put on new clothes. Gifts are exchanged among friends. Great family parties are arranged. And in many cities great fairs are opened to mark the end of the Fast of Ramadan.

Festival of the Sacrifice ('Id al-Adha)

Of all the prophets and leaders in the Old Testament, the patriarch Abraham and the lawgiver Moses are the most prominent. Yet neither the Jews nor the Christians celebrate their birthdays or any events in their lives. But the Moslems remember them in their holidays, as they remember Adam, Noah, Joseph and David, and many of the great Jewish prophets.

Noah's landing safely after the Flood is celebrated in the Festival of Ashura.

Adam's birthday is celebrated every Friday and is called Yaum al-jum'ah. The Moslems have no day of rest exactly like the Jewish Sabbath or the Lord's Day of the Christians. But Friday has been solemnized by special prayers and the Koran enjoins the True Believers to remember Allah on this day and "leave off bargaining." Friday has been chosen because on this day God created Adam. It is Adam's Birthday; and it is also the day when Adam was taken up to Paradise.

The Moslems of Palestine celebrate each year an elaborate Feast of the Prophet Moses, called 'Id Nebi Mussa. A great procession is led from Jerusalem to the shrine of Moses located near Jericho. A green velvet banner with its embroidery in gold, the banner of Nebi Mussa, leads the procession. Banners of many Mohammedan leaders are carried; and the banner bearers are followed by bands of musicians. Behind them come the singers and the dancers. The leader of the singers swings a sword or a stick to which a handkerchief has been tied, and his followers punctuate the singing with rhythmic clapping of the hands. After some days of festivity, the paraders return from the shrine of Moses to Jerusalem.

The best remembered and most joyously celebrated of the Old Testament characters is Abraham, Father Abraham. For the Moslems believe that Mohammed was a direct descendant of this patriarch.

The Koran retells in great detail the story of Abraham, son of Terah, who lived nearly two thousand years before the days of Jesus. Abraham had two wives. The name of one was Hagar, and the name of the other was Sarah. Hagar had a son, called Ishmael; and Sarah had a son whose name was Isaac.

The children of Israel, son of Isaac, son of Abraham, multiplied into the people called Jews. And the children of Ishmael, son of Abraham, multiplied into the people called Arabs.

When Ishmael was still very young, so the Moslems relate, God came to Abraham and asked him to take his beloved son and sacrifice him upon an altar. So great was Abraham's faith that whatever God asked him to do he he was ready to carry out. But just as he prepared to sacrifice his son Ishmael, a voice from heaven stayed the father's hand. Abraham looked about him and he saw a ram whose horns were entangled in the bushes; and he sacrificed the ram instead of his son.

This event is commemorated in Islam in a holiday called The Festival, or 'Id al-Adha, which arrives on the tenth day of the twelfth Moslem month; and it lasts for three days. Special prayers are prescribed for these days in re-

A CEMETERY IN NORTH AFRICA

membrance of the near-sacrifice of Ishmael. The days are spent in great festivities. But they are also kept as a time for the remembrance of the dead, and could be called the Moslem Memorial Days. People visit the burial grounds and decorate the graves of their families with palms. It is also customary for the women to bring food to the graveyard to distribute among the poor. Certain sections of the Koran are recited. The men usually go home after the ceremonies are over. But the women remain for the entire day; and some even spend the night at the graveyard.

During this Festival of the Sacrifice the main events in the childhood of Ishmael, ancestor of all the Arabs, and founder of the sacred city, Mecca, are related to the children.

When Ishmael was very, very young, so the legend runs, Sarah, who was jealous of Hagar, prevailed upon Abraham to drive Hagar and her son out of his tent. Hagar wandered off into the desert near the Red Sea, and there she and her child almost perished from thirst. Seven times Hagar ran from Mount Safā to Mount Maret and back, but she could find no well. Then Ishmael kicked the sand with his foot, and a spring of fresh water gushed out of the dry sand and saved their lives. This spring, now called the Zemzem, or the Well of Ishmael, was not very far from the place that Adam the First had marked as the center of the earth with the black stone he brought with him from the Garden of Eden.

Hagar settled with her son in that area, and a great city grew up around the sacred Zemzem and the shrine, called the Kaaba, which contains the black stone. In that city, many centuries later, was born the Prophet of Allah, Mohammed. Long before he was born, Arabs from many lands came to the sacred city to worship at the sacred stone brought from Paradise by Adam, and to drink of the waters of the Well of Ishmael. But Mohammed has made the pilgrimage to Mecca one of the Pillars of the Moslem Faith.

The Pilgrimage

Some holidays are observed every week; such are the Sabbath of the Jews, the Lord's Day of the Christians, and Adam's Birthday, which is kept by the Moslems.

There are some observances which are kept each month, like the Blessing of the New Moon of the Orthodox Jews.

Most holidays come once each year. They may last for only one day, as most Christian holidays do; or they may last two weeks, like the Chinese New Year; or they may continue for a full month, like the Fast of Ramadan.

But there is one religious holiday, observed by the Moslems, that comes for most of them only once in a lifetime. It is known as the Pilgrimage — the Fifth Pillar of Islam.

The reason for the Pilgrimage, the time of the Pilgrimage, the ritual to be observed by each pilgrim upon reaching the holy city, Mecca — all these are described in the Koran almost as fully as the sin offering of ignorance is described in Leviticus of the Old Testament.

Nor is anyone permitted to keep another from making the Pilgrimage. For the Koran says:

> Those who shall disbelieve and obstruct the way of God, and hinder men from visiting the Holy Mosque of Mecca, which God had appointed for a place to worship unto all men; and whosoever shall seek impiously to profane it, God will cause him to taste a grievous torment.

There are few in Islam who would hinder others from making the Pilgrimage; and millions of True Believers make every effort to carry out the Pilgrimage as soon as it is possible for them to arrange it.

Every year hundreds of thousands of Moslems make their way to Mecca, the city that is as holy to them as Rome is to devout Catholics and Jerusalem to Orthodox Jews. They come from all directions. They come from Yemen and Ethiopia, Egypt and Turkey, Oman and Iran, and from faraway India and the remotest parts of Africa, or wherever else Moslems live. They come by sea, as far as they can travel by sea. And the rest of the way to the Saudi Arabian holy city they travel by car, in camel caravans, on foot, or in airplanes.

And every pilgrim plans to reach Mecca before the seventh day of the month called Dhul-hijja, when the services and ritual of the Pilgrimage begin.

The Awe and the Wonder

On reaching a place within six miles of Mecca the pilgrims must stop for the preparation and dedication each must make before advancing another step. Mecca must be entered in a state of purity. Therefore each pilgrim must first bathe ritually, say the prescribed prayers, and put on special garments to be worn throughout the stay in Mecca. These garments are two white linen or cotton sheets which are draped about the body in a fixed way. Men must enter Mecca barefooted and bareheaded; women must have their faces covered in such a way that the veils do not touch the skin. Men and women must keep apart until the Pilgrimage festival is over.

Now they are ready to leave the profane world and enter on the sacred ground. The pilgrims proceed to Mecca. When they reach the spot where they can see the city and the Great Mosque, those seeing the sight for the first time begin to weep and moan. They look with awe upon the place they believe to be the center of the earth and the center of the universe. There are several sacred buildings in the great courtyard, enclosed by ornate colonnades. But the eyes of the pilgrims remain fixed on the structure called the Kaaba, which rises in the center to a height of about fifty feet, marking the spot where Adam dwelt.

For, according to legend, when Adam was banished from the Garden of Eden, he was heartbroken. To com-

THE KAABA

fort him, God set down a red tent on this spot; and here
Adam dwelt for the rest of his days. When Adam died, he
was buried nearby. And the Ruby from Heaven, called the
Black Stone, which Adam brought with him from Paradise, was later set into the wall of the Kaaba when this
shrine was built by Abraham and Ishmael.

The True Believers are awed and shaken as they approach this place. And they cry out:

"Here I am, O my God. here I am!"

"I am here to serve you, O my God, I am here to serve you!"

And then they proceed to the Great Mosque.

The Ten Rites

Ten rites are performed by each pilgrim during the Pilgrimage:

1. ENTRANCE THROUGH THE GATE OF PEACE. Nineteen gates lead into the great and sacred courtyard of the Great Mosque of Mecca. The courtyard is about 550 feet long and 360 feet wide, though each side is slightly different in length and width from the others. The newly arrived pilgrims must enter through the *Bab a-Salam*, the Gate of Peace.

2. THE KISSING OF THE BLACK STONE. Without tarrying, the pilgrim must make his way to the center of the courtyard where the Kaaba, a structure of about forty feet in length and thirty-three feet in width, rises to a height of about fifty feet. This shrine, built of reddish granite, has only one door, which leads into the unfurnished interior. The door is opened on special occasions each year. Into the eastern corner of the Kaaba, about five feet above the ground, is set a stone less than a foot across. This is the sacred Black Stone, the Ruby from Heaven. The walls of the Kaaba are always covered with black brocade curtains, which are changed every year.

The pilgrim who has just entered through the Gate
of Peace into the courtyard walks directly to the Kaaba,
and he kisses the Black Stone reverently. So many millions
of believers have done this in the past that the stone is
worn smooth.

3. THE CIRCUMBULATION. This is a hard word, but all
it means is "going around." After kissing the Black Stone,
the pilgrim must go around the Kaaba seven times, counter-
clockwise, keeping the shrine always to his left. The first
three rounds are made on the run; the last four rounds
are made slowly. Each time the Black Stone is passed, it is
kissed or touched with the fingertips.

After the seventh circling the worshiper presses himself
or herself against the wall of the shrine not far from the
door, to receive the blessing of virtue.

4. THE PRAYER AT THE MOSQUE OF ABRAHAM. The next
stage in the pilgrim's journey leads him to the small domed
Mosque of Abraham, which enshrines the graves of Ishmael
and his mother, Hagar. Here the pilgrim prays, then walks
over to the Well of Ishmael, the Zemzem, for a drink of
its sacred waters.

5. THE ASCENT TO MOUNT SAFĀ AND MOUNT MARET.
Now the pilgrim leaves the Mosque of Abraham, left foot
forward. He goes out of the courtyard through the Gate
of Safā, and follows a marked road leading from the hill-
top of Safā to the top of another hill called Marwa or
Maret. The distance between them is about a seventh of a
mile. The pilgrim must run back and forth between the

THE MAHMAL
Containing a new Holy
Curtain for the Kaaba

two elevations seven times, stopping at fixed stages for given prayers. This rite commemorates Hagar's seven-time search for water between Mount Safā and Mount Maret.

6. JOURNEY TO THE MOUNTAIN OF MERCY. On the eighth day of the twelfth month the pilgrims listen to a sermon near the Kaaba, and they receive instructions about the ceremonies of the following two days.

Early the next day the pilgrims start out on a long journey to Mount Arafat, several miles away. The number of pilgrims that reach Mount Arafat, the Mountain of Mercy, is always exactly 700,000 according to legend. If the number of men and women is smaller, angels come down to fill in the ranks.

7. THE SERMON ON ARAFAT. Another rite and duty during the Pilgrimage is fulfilled in listening to a sermon on Mount Arafat, delivered by a religious leader or a dignitary, always mounted on a camel.

8. THE NIGHT IN MUZDALIFA. That evening the pilgrims return to Mecca. Midway between Arafat and Mecca, the pilgrims remain for the night in Muzdalifa. No one goes to sleep that night. Crowds gather at the Mosque of Muzdalifa. Music is played. And the pilgrims go out in search of pebbles for their next rite. Each one gathers seventy pebbles.

9. THE STONING OF THE DEVILS IN MINA. The next day, on their return journey to Mecca, the pilgrims stop in the village of Mina. Here there are three pillars at which the pilgrims throw their pebbles in a ceremony called the

THE NIGHT IN MUZDALIFA

Stoning of the Devils. And they shout: "There is no god but Allah!"

10. THE VISIT TO THE TOMB OF MOHAMMED. The pilgrims return to Mecca, where many try to obtain a bottle or tin of water from the Well of Ishmael. They take the water home for relatives or to keep and use in time of illness.

Then the pilgrims make their way some two hundred miles to Medina, the city of the Prophet, to visit the tomb of Mohammed.

And the Pilgrimage is over.

Those Moslems who cannot make the Pilgrimage at the prescribed time may make it any time during the year, following the same ritual, and that is known as the Lesser Pilgrimage.

Only Moslems are permitted to enter Mecca. But in the past a number of non-Moslems have disguised themselves as pilgrims and have returned to relate what they observed. Those who are caught in this deception face the death penalty.

The Pilgrimage is the most important event in the religious life of the Moslem.

VII   OTHER
HOLIDAYS

The Names Are Different

Many of the religious holidays that have been described in this book appear in different lands, sometimes under different names, and sometimes are kept on different dates or celebrated with different ceremonies. East European Jews, for instance, keep the Sabbath quite differently from American Jews. Christmas is observed by all Christians, but not on the same day or in the same way. The Buddhist holidays appear under different names and are celebrated with different ceremonies in Ceylon and in Burma, in Tibet and in Japan.

In Japan the Buddhist holidays take on a Japanese character. They are observed in much the same way as the holidays the Japanese keep in honor of their emperors. For the Japanese believe that their emperors are of divine origin, and that their first emperor, Jimmu Tenno, was the grandson of the sun goddess Amaterasu-Omi-Kami.

In Nepal the holidays are mainly Buddhist and Hindu. But the Nepalese celebrate them differently from the rest of India, or China. They have given their holidays a national character, and have somehow interwoven them with the great events in their history.

In Siam and in Tibet the holidays are also mainly Buddhist, but they are observed with a pageantry and colorful ritual unknown in other Buddhist countries.

Then there are some living religions with very small followings who have holidays of their own as precious to them as ours are to us.

The Parsi Holidays

One of the world's truly great religions is Zoroastrianism, which was founded in Iran long ago by a leader named Zoroaster. Exactly when Zoroaster was born we really do not know. Some people claim that he was born a little over 2600 years ago; and others maintain that he existed 5000 years earlier than that. But all are agreed that he was an Iranian who left the world a great heritage in his teachings.

For Zoroaster taught that the world is ruled by Two

Principles or Forces. They are unlike the positive and negative Principles of the Chinese, which are neither good nor
bad. The Two Forces preached by Zoroaster are: Ahura

A PARSI HIGH PRIEST

*Placing chips of sandalwood on a fire-holder; offerings are
flowers, food, milk, wine and water*

Mazda, the spirit of good; and Angra Manyu, the spirit of
evil. These two forces are forever at war over the hearts
of men. And he who wishes to enlist on the side of good
against evil can help in three ways: he can do good deeds;

he can speak good words; and he can think good thoughts. These three are called "the Way of the Good Spirit."

The teachings of Zoroaster are written down in the Avesta, the sacred scriptures of the Zoroastrians, some of whom live in Iran, and the rest in India. The followers of this religion are called Parsi in India to indicate that this religion came originally from Persia.

The Zoroastrians, about 100,000 of them, celebrate Zoroaster's birthday each year. And each year, late in March, they observe the New Year, which they call Nauruz, or Navroz.

They have other and some quite strange holidays. One is the Feast of Muttering, called Zamzamah; another is the Feast of the Water Lily, Casn-i Nilufar; and the most curious of them all is Sir-Sava, the Garlic Feast, when they eat this vegetable to keep away evil spirits.

Holidays of the Jains

In India there dwell about 2,000,000 people who follow a religion called the Faith of the Conquerors, Jainism. But they are quite the opposite of people who go out to conquer others. They devote their lives to conquering themselves. Like all other religions, Jainism has commandments by which to live the good life. These commandments say: Do not steal; do not lie; do not covet; do not get drunk; and so on. But their first commandment, called Ahimsa, is the most important. This commandment tells them: *Do not kill any living thing, nor ever hurt any living thing by deed, word, or thought.*

That means that the followers of this religion cannot eat meat. They are all vegetarians. They cannot kill or hurt even mosquitoes or wild animals.

The Jains cannot go to war or strike back at anyone who attacks them, man or beast. They cannot become soldiers, and they cannot become farmers — for farmers plowing and harrowing must kill worms and insects. The Jains cannot engage in work that might cause the death of any living thing, down to the lowliest of insects.

Once each year, "one month and twenty nights" after the rainy season in India, the Jains observe an eight-day fast — the Fast of Pajjusana, when they confess their sins against Ahimsa and repent any harm they may have done to any living thing, consciously or unconsciously.

The Jains also observe a kind of Sabbath, called Posaha. They do not keep it each week, but twice each lunar month, on the new moon and the full moon. On these two Posaha days the Jains do not go to work, they do not eat, they do not bathe, they use no incense. They spend these days in prayer and in reading the Agamas, their sacred scriptures.

VIII THE WORLD'S NEWEST HOLIDAY

Have you noticed anything?

Most of the holidays of the world concern the joy of living and the sweetness of freedom.

People rejoice in the coming of spring and the bounty of autumn. They commemorate deliverance from disasters, such as floods and epidemics. They celebrate their emancipation from slavery, or securing their independence from tyranny. They honor ancestors who fought on the side of good against evil, on the side of justice against injustice, on the side of honesty against corruption.

That is what the holidays of the world are mainly about.

And people learned long ago that if man is to have the joy of living and the sweetness of freedom it must first come to all mankind. In practically all the holidays, in the ritual or in the prayers that belong with them, we find the hope for peace and the Brotherhood of Man. "Peace on earth; good will to men!" This sentiment appears in different forms during the holidays, everywhere.

Religious leaders have dreamed of universal peace and the brotherhood of man for many, many centuries. A great prophet of old foretold the time when the nations of the earth "shall beat their swords into plowshares, and their spears into pruninghooks: nation shall not lift up a sword against nation, neither shall they learn war any more. But they shall sit every man under his vine and under his fig tree; and none shall make them afraid."

Yet it was not until our own times that the principle was established that all nations should live together in peace, as a United Nations.

United Nations Day

In April, 1945, representatives of fifty nations met in the United States, in the city of San Francisco, to draw up a document now known as the Charter of the United Nations.

Six months later, on the twenty-fourth day of October, the United Nations Charter was adopted and approved by the majority of the countries that took part in preparing the laws to govern this new world organization. As of that day the United Nations was officially in existence!

The functions of the United Nations are many; but the purposes or aims are very few.

The aims of the United Nations, according to its Charter, are:

To promote peace and to prevent war;

To promote equality between people and nations, regardless of race, color, or sex;

And to nourish faith in justice and in freedom, the world over.

These aims are the soul and essence of the United Nations.

For most of the nations on earth to have accepted these principles of the United Nations, after so many centuries of strife, marks one of the greatest triumphs of the human spirit. It deserves to be celebrated by all of mankind.

And that is actually what has happened. On October 31, 1947, in the one hundred and first plenary meeting of the General Assembly of the United Nations, it was declared that October 24, the anniversary of the coming into force of the Charter of the United Nations, should be observed as United Nations Day.

In less time than "a mustard seed can stand on the pointed edge of a cow's horn," as the Hindus put it, the idea traveled around the world.

United Nations Day is now observed in practically all

the countries that already belong to the United Nations. On this day church bells ring at noon in many places, and locomotives blow their whistles. Special prayers for peace and brotherhood are said in many churches of different faiths. The United Nations flag is raised ceremoniously in public squares and over public buildings.

In some places, as in Bolivia for instance, United Nations Day is a school holiday. But in most places pupils are kept in school to celebrate the observance of this day. The pupils raise the flag of the United Nations over the school. And the day is devoted to explanations of the meaning of the day, the showing of films that portray what the United Nations has achieved so far, and in assembly dancing and singing.

Everywhere there are posters of the blue-and-white United Nations flag. In some cities thousands of students parade with the United Nations flag and the flags of all the member nations. They sing songs of peace and brotherhood. And they dance in the public squares.

Letters going through the mail on October 24, whether in Argentina or Australia, Bolivia or Honduras, Mexico or Pakistan, all have the stamps canceled with the words "United Nations Day," each in the language of that country.

Though this day has been declared by some governments to be an official holiday, in most countries it is still merely an observance. The United Nations is still very, very young. As the United Nations grows older and stronger, and its aims are accepted by all the people on earth, United Nations Day will become a full-fledged holiday.

It will be the first of the Brotherhood of Man holidays.

It will be the world's newest of the Great Holidays.

And it will be a truly "around the world" holiday.

THE FLAG OF THE UNITED NATIONS

PRINCIPAL HOLIDAYS
OBSERVED IN
THE UNITED STATES

New Year's Day *	January 1
Lincoln's Birthday	February 12
Saint Valentine's Day *	February 14
Washington's Birthday	February 22
Good Friday *	Friday before Easter
Easter *	Sunday — usually early in April
May Day *	May 1
Memorial Day	May 30
Independence Day	July 4
Labor Day	First Monday in September
Columbus Day	October 12
Halloween *	October 31
All Saints' Day *	November 1
Armistice Day	November 11
Thanksgiving Day *	Fourth Thursday in November
Christmas *	December 25

*Denotes that the holiday is treated in this book

ACKNOWLEDGMENTS

I am indebted to Miss Grace Yang of the China Institute of America for reading the section on "The Chinese Holidays" and for her valuable comments. I am similarly indebted to Dr. Moni Moulik, Director of the India Information Services, and Mr. Gyanendra Prasad Jain, Research Officer of the Embassy of India in Washington, for their comments on "The Hindu Holidays"; to Dr. Abraham E. Millgram, Education Director of the United Synagogue Commission on Jewish Education, and Dr. Emanuel Gamoran, Director of Education for the Union of American Hebrew Congregations, for their reading and suggestions on "The Jewish Holidays"; to Miss Mary Tully of the Union Theological Seminary, for her reactions to "The Christian Holidays"; to Dr. Edwin E. Calverley, Editor of *The Muslim World*, for his reading of the section on

"The Moslem Holidays"; and to Dr. V. J. G. Stavridi, Director of Extension Services of the United Nations, for supplying material for "The World's Newest Holiday."

It gives me pleasure to express here my gratitude to the librarians of the Union Theological Seminary, the Jewish Theological Seminary, and the Missionary Research Library for their helpfulness when this book was in preparation.

J. G.

INDEX

(C) Chinese
(J) Jewish
(M) Moslem

(H) Hindu
(Chr) Christian
(Z) Zoroastrian

ABRAHAM, the patriarch, 90, 95; in Moslem belief, 180
Adam's birthday, 94, 179
Aditi, mother of the gods, 77
Adoration of the Magi, 164
Advent (Chr), 164
Agamas, Jainist sacred scriptures, 196
Age of the Vedas, 61
Ahimsa, 195–196
Ahura Mazda, 194
All Saints' Day (Chr), 154–157
All Souls' Day (Chr), 158
Allahabad, City of God, 57
Allhallow Eve. *See* Halloween
Almanac (C), 26
Altair, the Falling Star, 38–40
Amaterasu-Omi-Kami, 193
Amulets (H), 73
Ancestor worship, 16, 34
Ancestors, souls of, 13
Angra Manyu, 194
Animals, sacred (H), 72
Anno Hegira, 169
Arafat, Mount, 189
Around-the-world holiday, 201
Ash marks (H), 84
Ash Wednesday (Chr), 145
Ashura (M), 172
Avatar (H), 60–61
Avesta, Zoroastrian teachings, 195

Bab a-Salam, 187
Bagdad, 170
Balabhadra, Krishna's brother, 63
Bali Worship Day (H), 72.
Basanta (H), 81–82
Bethlehem, 135, 136
Birthday of the Moon (C), 10, 43–44
Birthday of the Prophet (M), 173
Birthday of the Sun (C), 42–43
Black Stone, 186, 187, 188
Blessing of the Wine (J), 92, 97
Boat races (C), 36
Bonfires of Holi (H), 83–84
Book of Esther, 112
Book of Life, 96, 168
Brahma, the Creator, 54, 61
Bridegroom of Genesis (J), 105
Bridegroom of the Torah (J), 105
Bride Sabbath, 93
Brotherhood of Man, 11; holiday, 201
Buddha, 15, 173
Buddhism, 15
Burial ground (C), 33

CALENDAR (H), 54; (J), 91; (M), 172–173
Candlemas (Chr), 164
Casn-i Nilufar (Z), 195
Celebration of a Miracle (J), 106–109

Cerelia, Roman holiday, 160
Ceres, Roman goddess, 159–160
Chariot festival (H), 64
Ching Che (C), 16
Ch'ing Ming (C), 10, 30–31
Christians in India, 53
Christ Mass, 133
Christmas (Chr), 10, 130–137; tree, 131, 134–135; Eve, 132–133; carols, 132; Day, 134
Christ's baptism, 164
Ch'u Yuan (C), 35–38
Chung Yang Chieh (C), 10, 48–51
Ci'ien Niu, 38
Circle of Happiness, 45
Circumbulation (M), 188
City of God, Allahabad, 57
Confirmation, day of (J), 129
Confucianism, 15
Confucius, teachings of, 15, 16
Constantine, Emperor of Rome, 133
Crossing the Milky Way, 40

Dasáratha, King (H), 70
Dawn goddess (H), 61
Day, lunar, 6
Day of Atonement (J), 98–100
Day of Great Help (J), 103
Days, names of the, 8
Devaki, Princess, 62
Dhana Trayodashi (H), 72
Dhvajaropana (H), 57–59
Dipavali. *See* Diwali
Diwali (H), 56, 71–72
Dragon Boat Festival (C), 35–38
Dragon parade (C), 28–29
Dragon Play (C), 21, 28
Durga Puja (H), 10, 65–70
Dussera (H), 69–71

Easter (Chr), 10, 145–152; lilies, 148–149; eggs, 149–151; Monday, 152
Egg, as symbol, 150

Egg rolling (Chr), 150–151
Egyptian day, 6
Eight Immortals (C), 13
Elements, the five (C), 18
Emperor Claudius, 142
Eostur, goddess of spring, 146
Epiphany (Chr), 164
Equinox, 7
Even number (C), 33; (H), 83

Faith of the Conquerors, 195
Falling Star Altair, 38–39
Family holidays, 3
Fast, of Ramadan (M), 175–177; of Pajjusana (Jain), 196
Fatima (M), 170
Feast of, the Lanterns (C), 28–29; Esther (J), 110–120; the Blessed Virgin Mary (Chr), 164; the Circumcision of Jesus (Chr), 164; the Holy Innocents (Chr), 164; Saint John (Chr), 164; Saint Stephen (Chr), 164; the Prophet Moses (M), 179; the Water Lily (Z), 195; Muttering (Z), 195
Fei-Ch'ang-Fang, the magician, 48
Festival of, the Tragic Lovers (C), 38–40, 48; Liberation (C), 44; Reunion (C), 44; the Great Bear (H), 54; the Divine Mother (H), 65–70; the Garland of Lights (H), 71–72; Tools (H), 79–80; Booths (J), 100–105; Janus (Roman), 137; Ashura (M), 179; the Sacrifice (M), 179
Fire Festival (H), 81–86
Fire God (H), 61
First Feast of the Dead (C), 34
First of Muharram (M), 168
Five, in Chinese symbolism, 18
Five Books of Moses, 104
Five-in-one holiday (H), 73–74
Five K's of Jainism, 53
Five Pillars of Faith (M), 175–177

Flora, Roman goddess, 152
Fourth Commandment, 91

GANESHA, 65
Ganga Puja (H), 10
Ganges, sacred river, 57–58
Garland of Lights (H), 71–72
Garlic Feast (Z), 195
Gate of, Peace, 187; Safā, 188
Gauri, 79
Gautama Buddha, 15, 173
Goddess of smallpox, 59–60
Good luck painting (H), 74
Great Celebration (J), 120–125
Great Mosque, 185
Great Yang (T'ai Yang), 12
Great Yin (T'ai Yin), 13
Gregorian calendar, 164
Guru Nanak, 53

HADASSAH, called Esther, 114
Hagar, 180, 183, 188
Halloween, 155–157
Haman, 114–119
Hamishah Osar Bish'vat (J), 109–110
Han Lu (C), 17
Han Shih (C), 30
Hanukkah (J), 106–109
Hanuman (H), 55, 71
Harvest festivals, 163
High Holy Days (J), 94–100
Hindu Minerva, 65
Hinduism, 53
Holi (H), 81–86
Holiday of, the Alligator (H), 58; Incarnations (H), 60–64; Tabernacles (J), 100; Seven Weeks (J), 127–128; First Fruits (J), 128
Holika, 85–86
Holy Fair of Allahabad, 58
Holy Scrolls (J), 98, 105
Honey, in Jewish symbolism, 129
Hoshana Rabah (J), 103, 104

House of, Aries, 56; Capricorn, 56; Makara, 57
H'sia Chih (C), 17
Huan Ching, 48, 49
Husain, Hazrat Imam, 170–171

'ID AL-ADHA (M), 179, 181
Id-al-Fitr (M), 178
'Id Nebi Mussa (M), 179
Image of, Durga, 66; Saraswati, 82
India, land of many religions, 52
Isaac, the patriarch, 90, 95
Ishmael, ancestor of the Arabs, 180
Islam, 166

JACOB, the patriarch, 90, 95
Jade Emperor, 22, 39
Jagannath. See Juggernaut
Jainism, 52, 195
Janmashtami (H), 62–64
Janus, god of agriculture, 137, 138
Japanese holidays, 192–193
Jatakas, 173
Jesus, birthday of, 133
Jimmu Tenno, 193
Jubilee number, 127
Judas Maccabeus, 107–108
Juggernaut, 63–64
Julius Caesar, 137, 164
Jumna river, 57

KAABA, Moslem shrine, 183, 185–186, 188
Kalika Purana, Hindu sacred book, 78
Karma, the law of life (H), 60
Karttikeya, 65–66
Kerbela, 169–171
King of the Day, 41–42
King of the Seas, 174
Kitchen God (C), 22, 24
Kiteflying Holiday (C), 48–51
Kojagari Purnima (H), 10
Koran (M), 166, 169, 176, 177
Kowtow, 26, 42

Krishna (H), 62–64
Krishnavatara (H), 60–64
Kriss Kringle, 135

LABOR DAY, 80
Lag B'omer (J), 125–126
Lakshmi, 65, 72, 74–76
Lanterns, Feast of the (C), 28–29
Lao-tse, 15–16
Leap year months (J), 90–91
Lent (Chr), forty days of, 145–146
Li Chum (C), 17–20
Lord Tsin, 31
Lord's Day (Chr), 94
Luck, bad (C), 27; omen, 32
Lucky, signs (C), 21; days (H), 87–88
Lunar, month, 6; year (C), 14; year (J), 90; year (M), 166
Lupercalia, Roman holiday, 141
Luperus, the Wolf Killer, 141
Luther, Martin, 134–135

MACCABEES, 107
Mahabharata, Hindu epic, 62
Mahishaur, Hindu demon, 67
Makara Sankranti (H), 56–58
Man in the Moon, 46–48
Mantras, 63
Maret, Mount, 188, 189
Mass of Christ, 133
May Day, 154
Maypoles, 152–153
Mecca, 169, 185, 189
Medina, city of, 191
Memorial Day, 159; (C), 32–34
Meron, pilgrimage to, 126
Milky Way, in Chinese legend, 39
Miracle, in a cruse of oil, 109; of Cana, 164
Mohammed, 166, 169, 173–175
Mohammedans, 166
Moon, dwellers, 45; Rabbit, 45; Toad, 45; Queen, 46; birthday of, 43–44, 48

Mordecai, 114, 116
Moses, 92, 111, 173
Moslem Era, 169
Moslems, in Pakistan, 53, 167; in Africa, 167; in Asia, 167; in Egypt, 167; in Iran, 167
Mosque of Abraham, 188
Mother's Day (H), 69
Mountain of Mercy, 189
Muharram (M), 166–172
Muzdalifa, Mosque of, 189

NARAKA CHATURDASHI (H), 77
Narakarasura, demon (H), 72, 77, 78
National holidays, 3
Nature worship, 9, 16
Navroz (Z), 195
Neem tree, 59
New Year, of Business (H), 72, 75; of the Trees (J), 109–110
New Year's Day (C), 24; (H), 56–60; (J), 94–96; (Chr), 137–141; (M), 168; (Z), 195

OCTAVE OF CHRISTMAS, 164
Odd numbers (C), 33

PAKISTAN, Moslems in, 53, 167
Palatine Hill, 142
Palm Sunday (Chr), 146
P'an Ku, the Chinese Adam, 37
Parade, for Li Chum, 18; of the lanterns, 29
Paradise, boundary of, 168
Parsi faith, 52
Passion Week (Chr), 146
Passover (J), 120–125
Pentecost (J), 126–129; (Chr), 164
Pilgrimage, to Puri, 63–64; to Mecca, 175–191
Posaha, Jainist Sabbath, 196
Procession of, the Chariots (H), 64; the Scrolls (J), 105

Prophet of Allah, 183
Pure and Bright Festival (C), 30–31
Purim (J), 110–120
Puritans, on May Day, 154

QUEEN OF HEAVEN, 44
Queen of the Night, 41–42

RAIN GOD (H), 61
Rakhi Bandhana (H), 73
Rakhi Purnima. See Rakhi Bandhana
Ram Lila, Hindu pageant, 70
Rama, 70–71
Ramayana, Hindu epic, 70
Ratha Yathra (H), 56
Ravana, Hindu demon, 70–71
Red Cock, 42
Religious holidays, 4
Resurrection, legend of the (Chr), 147–148
Rishi Panchami (H), 54
Ritual bathing (H), 76; (M), 185
Romulus and Remus, 142
Rosh Hashonoh (J), 94–96
Ruby from Heaven (M), 186

SABBATH (J), 91–93
Safā, Mount, 188, 189
Saint Nicholas, 135
Saint Valentine's Day, 141–145
Santa Claus, 131, 135
Saraswati, Hindu Minerva, 65, 81–83
Saturn, Roman god, 133
Saturnalia, 133, 134
Scholar's Day (J), 125–126
Seder, pageant of (J), 121–124
Sesamum seed, 58
Seven, symbolism of (J), 126–127
Seven Immortals (H), 55
Shabuoth (J), 10, 126–129
Shamini Atzereth (J), 104
Shashti, evil goddess (H), 79

Shrove Tuesday (Chr), 154
Shushan, 112
Sikh religion, 53
Sikhs, 53
Simchath Torah (J), 104–105
Simeon Bar Yohai, 125–126
Sinai, Mount, 127, 128
Sir-Sava (Z), 195
Sitala, 59–60
Siva, the Destroyer, 54, 61
Solemn Days (J), 94–100
Solstice, 7
Spirit of Thanksgiving, 10
Star of Bethlehem, 136
Stoning of Devils (M), 189
Succah, 101–103
Succoth (J), 10, 100–105
Subhadra (H), 63
Sun god (H), 61
Sweethearts' holiday, 142

TAMOOSA, King of the Seas, 174
Taoism, 15
Ten Commandments, 91, 127–128
Ten-day holiday (M), 167
Ten days of Repentance (J), 94–100
Ten Rites (M), 187–190
Teng Chieh (C), 28–29
Thanksgiving (J), 101–103; origin in the United States, 159–161
Threading of the Needle Holiday, 41
Three-in-One-God (H), 54, 61
Three-in-one holiday (C), 34
Toad, three-legged, 45
Tomb of Mohammed, 190–191
Torah Festival (J), 104–105
Tree of Life, 169
Tree Planting Festival (C), 34
Triad (H), 61
Trimurti: Three-in-One-God (H), 54, 61
T'sao Wang, Chinese god, 22
Tuan Wu (C), 35–38
T'wan Yuan Chieh (C), 44

Two Creative Principles (C), 12, 13, 28, 33, 37
Two Forces (Z), 193–194

UMBRIANS, 6
United Nations Day, 198–201
Unlucky days (H), 87–88

VASHTI, QUEEN, 113
Vasudeva, Prince, 62
Vedic Age, 61
Vega, 38–40
Vishnu, the Preserver (H), 54, 56, 61, 62–64, 77
Visvakarma, Hindu god, 79
Visvakarma Puja (H), 79–80

WELL OF ISHMAEL, 182, 183, 188
Whitsunday (Chr), 164

YAMA HOLIDAY (H), 72, 73
Yang and Yin (C), 12, 28, 33, 37
Yathrib, 169
Yaum al-jum'ah (M), 179
Year, lunar (C), 14; (J), 90; (M), 166
Ying, province of, 35
Yom Kippur (J), 98–100
Yozid, Husain's enemy, 170
Yu Shui (C), 16
Yueh Lao Yeh, 47–48

ZAMZAMAH (Z), 195
Zarathustra. See Zoroaster
Zemzem. See Well of Ishmael
Zeresh, 116–117
Zoroaster, 52, 173, 193–195
Zoroastrianism, 52, 193–195